MODERN WORLD NATIONS

AFGHANISTAN
AUSTRIA
BAHRAIN
BERMUDA
CHINA
CUBA
EGYPT
ETHIOPIA
REPUBLIC OF GEORGIA
GERMANY
KUWAIT
IRAN
IRAQ
ISRAEL
MEXICO
NEW ZEALAND
PAKISTAN
RUSSIA
SAUDI ARABIA
SCOTLAND
SOUTH KOREA
UKRAINE

MODERN WORLD NATIONS

Bahrain

Often called "the Pearl of the Persian Gulf," Bahrain is actually a group of islands connected by causeways. Before the beginning of the petroleum industry, the region's economy was fueled in part by an abundance of pearls gathered by divers from the surrounding seabed.

1

Introducing Bahrain

ahrain—the "Pearl of the Persian Gulf"—is the smallest and most densely populated Arab country. Its land area is only some 260 square miles (670 square kilometers), making it roughly the size of Chicago, Illinois, or one-fifth the area of tiny Rhode Island. Yet its nearly 700,000 people give this desert kingdom a population density of nearly 2,700 people per square mile (1,025 per square kilometer), making it one of the most crowded countries on Earth.

The country is formed by an *archipelago* (a group of islands), located midway along the western edge of the Persian Gulf (also called the Arabian Sea by many people living in the region).[1]

[1] Most Bahraini names have two spellings, the local Arabic one and one commonly used in the West. Throughout this book, the accepted English spelling is used.

Centuries ago, Arabs divided what is now known as the Persian Gulf into several smaller water bodies. *Bahrain* comes from an Arabic word meaning "two seas," referring to several of the smaller bodies of water that surround the country's 33 islands. Only 5 of these islands, however, are settled. Others are small and rocky, lack a fresh water supply, or are closed to the public; some islands even disappear beneath the sea during high tide!

Bahrain is the largest and most important island of the group and gave its name to the entire country. Even though it stretches only 27 miles (43 kilometers) north to south and is only a narrow 8 to 10 miles (13 to 16 kilometers) wide, Bahrain occupies over four-fifths of the country's total area, and is home to more than two-thirds of all Bahrainis.

Manama, the country's capital and largest city, is located on the island's northeastern tip. Causeways—raised highways built over water and low ground—connect the island to Al Muharraq, the second largest island and location of Bahrain's international airport, and to Sitrah, which is mainly an industrial area. Other inhabited islands are Nabih Saleh, Jiddah, and Umm Al-Nassan.

People have lived in Bahrain for a very long time. Its history goes back at least 50,000 years, to the dawn of modern-day humans. Such artifacts as flint tools indicate that agriculture—the very root of civilization—was practiced in Bahrain as early as 8000 B.C. Several thousand years later, during the third millennium B.C., this archipelago became the seat of the Dilmun civilization. This Bronze Age culture, with its strength based on a wealthy and powerful trading empire, lasted some 2,000 years. Dilmun culture and economy thrived because of the islands' strategic geographic location, lying along important trade routes linking Mesopotamia with the Indus Valley in present-day Pakistan.

Dilmun must have appeared to the weary traveler like a green oasis rising above the blue waters of the Persian Gulf.

Bahrain's capital, Manama, is also its largest city—a thriving metropolis whose skyline is highlighted by many modern hotels and office buildings.

Even today, those who first see Bahrain often remark on the amazing "mirage-like" sight of its modern cities and its lush, green farmlands that stand in stark contrast to their parched desert surroundings. Sumerians, an early people living in Mesopotamia who developed one of the world's earliest civilizations, believed that Dilmun was a holy island. And Babylonians, another early civilization that was centered in

Bahrain's rich history stretches back thousands of years. During the Bronze Age, the Dilmun civilization capitalized on the country's strategic location to build a powerful trading empire. Ruins of this once great civilization remain and attest to the enduring culture of the region.

the Tigris and Euphrates River Valleys of present-day Iraq, believed Dilmun was a place of eternal life, where heroes went when they died. Some scholars even believe that Bahrain may have been the place that inspired biblical references to the Garden of Eden.

You might be wondering why this small, remote, desert kingdom of Bahrain is called the Pearl of the Persian Gulf. The answer lies at the bottom of the sea. For centuries pearl gathering was the main occupation and source of income in Bahrain. In fact, pearl divers have been searching for and gathering these precious gems for at least 5,000 years. An ancient Sumerian tale, *The Epic of Gilgamesh,* describes a diver tying heavy stones to his feet to help his plunge to the sea floor. There he would pluck the "magic flowers" that form in oysters living on the seabed. However, many millennia later, at about the same time that oil was discovered in Bahrain, the global market for pearls collapsed due to the introduction of cheaper cultured (artificially grown) pearls from Japan. Although pearl diving is no longer an important economic activity, Bahraini pearls are still very valuable, and a few *dhows,* or small fishing boats, continue to bring them in.

Bahrain is the most popular tourist destination in the entire Persian Gulf region. Many things attract travelers to this smallest of all Arab states: Its government is stable, plus the country is strikingly modern, quite safe for visitors, and very liberal relative to many other nations in this very conservative region. Bahrain is also a country of many important "firsts." In 1932, for example, it was the first Arabian country bordering the Persian Gulf to find oil, a discovery that brought newfound prosperity to this tiny country. When Bahrain's neighbors all discovered petroleum, as well, each of them built nearly all of their economy on this single resource. But Bahrain refused to do so. Instead, it became the first country in the Persian Gulf region to begin diversifying its economy. In 1971, for instance, Bahrain started producing the lightweight metal, aluminum. And since then it has branched out into other economic activities to reduce its dependence on oil as its chief source of income.

Bahrain is also one of the most open Arab countries

with regard to the media. Many Arab states restrict the information that newspapers and radio and television stations are allowed to report. Bahrain, however, gives the press a great deal of freedom to report what it wants. The country's long history as a trading nation may be one reason why its people are so open and liberal. Long-term contact with various cultures over the course of many centuries has given Bahrain a business-oriented, trade-centered culture that is not afraid to interact with other people who have a different way of life.

Still another first for Bahrain is in the field of education. In 1919 the country established the first public-school system in the Persian Gulf region. Today all youngsters between the ages of 6 and 15 must attend school, and public education is free.

Many travelers come from neighboring Saudi Arabia. The 30-minute drive across the 15-mile-long (24 kilometers) King Fahd Causeway that links strict, conservative, and very traditional Saudi Arabia to Bahrain is like passage into another world. Bahrain is very Westernized. A traveler from the United States or Canada will see many billboards advertising familiar products that are very popular here; alcohol can be purchased both in stores and restaurants, neither of which is possible in other Islamic Arab countries, where alcohol is forbidden; a number of Western hotel chains have built modern beachfront resorts; and many merchants cater to Western tastes. There are even golf courses with grass fairways and greens. According to one visitor from tradition-bound Saudi Arabia, a trip to Bahrain is like "escaping to a little touch of America, or the West."

Although Bahrain is in a far-distant and culturally quite different part of the world, you can travel to and through this small, unique, and very interesting Pearl of the Persian Gulf by simply traveling the pages of this book. Have an enjoyable trip and adventure!

Bahrain is comprised of a group of low-lying islands located in the Persian Gulf between the Saudi Arabian mainland and the Qatar peninsula. The name *Bahrain* is derived from the Arabic for "two seas." Bahrain's strategic location has made it a commercial center for the Middle East.

Viewed from outer space, the islands of Bahrain can be seen in the western edge of the Persian Gulf sandwiched between peninsular Qatar and Saudi Arabia. The nation is composed of 33 islands, the largest of which are connected by causeways. Some of the smaller, unpopulated islands actually vanish beneath the Gulf during high tide.

Natural Landscapes

ahrain is located in the Persian Gulf only 15 miles (24 kilometers) from the eastern coast of Saudi Arabia and 17 miles (28 kilometers) northwest of Qatar. Its tiny area of only 267 square miles (692 square kilometers) is distributed among 33 islands. A fairly shallow inlet of the Persian Gulf, called the Gulf of Bahrain, surrounds much of the country. The gulf has well-developed coral reefs, particularly to the north of the large island of Bahrain. It also has large oyster beds that for thousands of years have been the source of the country's famous pearls.

Land Features

The islands that form Bahrain are the most significant land features. They are small, low lying, and under natural conditions covered mostly by a barren sandy or rocky desert surface. A few low-lying limestone hills and shallow water-cut (though usually dry) streambeds, called *wadis,* give some relief to an otherwise rather flat and featureless landscape. Three kinds of surface qualities characterize desert regions: sand, occasionally in the form of dunes; gravel, or "desert pavement"; and solid rock surfaces in which sand and gravel have been eroded (scoured out) by the work of wind or flowing water. Each of these three occurs in various areas of Bahrain. Much of the country is covered with salty sand that can support only a few very hardy, salt-tolerant plant species.

The largest and most important island, Bahrain (from which the country takes its name), occupies an area of about 220 square miles (570 square kilometers). Hardy thorn trees and scrub and a variety of other drought-resistant plants struggle to survive in this dry, salty sand. Other varieties of vegetation, including cultivated crops, are limited mainly to a fertile strip of land along the island's northern coast. A number of crops, including groves of date palms, almonds, figs, and pomegranate trees, thrive under irrigated conditions. The interior of the island has a promontory that rises to 440 feet (134 meters) before dropping abruptly as an escarpment (steep cliff). This feature, the highest point in the country, is named Jabal al Dukhan, or "Mountain of Smoke." It takes its name from the clouds and mist that often cling to its summit.

Manama, the capital city, is located on the northeastern tip of the island of Bahrain. Mina Salman, the country's chief seaport, also is located on the island. The major petroleum refining facilities and commercial centers can be found on this important island, too. Bahrain is connected to nearby islands and to the mainland of Saudi Arabia by a series of causeways and bridges. The oldest causeway was built in 1929 and links Bahrain to Al Muharraq, the second-largest island. Although Al Muharraq is only 3.75 miles (6 kilometers) long, the country's international airport is located there, as is

Bahrain's second largest city, likewise named Al Muharraq. A causeway also connects Al Muharraq to the tiny island of Jazirat al Azl, the site of a major ship-repair and dry-dock center. The country's chief oil export terminal is situated south of Jazirat al Azl on the island of Sitrah. This small island is linked to Bahrain by a bridge that spans the narrow channel separating the two islands. Off the northwestern coast of Bahrain is one of the country's larger islands, Umm an Nasan, which is the private property of the *emir* (ruler) and the site of his personal game preserve. It is located on the causeway that links the Saudi mainland town of Al Khobar to the island of Bahrain.

Other islands in the group include Nabi Salah, on which date palm groves are irrigated with water from the island's freshwater springs, and Jiddah, the small, rocky site of Bahrain's prison. Located south of Bahrain, near Qatar, is the island of Hawar and 15 much smaller adjacent islands. Although claimed by Bahrain, these islands are involved in a heated territorial dispute with Qatar, which also lays claim to them. The few remaining islands are uninhabited and of little importance, other than serving as nesting sites for a great variety of migratory birds.

Climate—A Land of Two Seasons

Bahrain has two seasons: an extremely hot, humid summer and a relatively mild and pleasant winter. During the summer season, extending from May through September, skies are mostly cloudless, and temperatures are constantly high, with afternoon temperatures almost always soaring above 100° F (38° C). In July, the hottest month, the afternoon highs reach a scorching average of 108° F (42° C)! Nighttime temperatures are also stifling hot, averaging 81° F (27 ° C) for the monthly average low temperature—making it one of the world's hottest night-time places. On rare occasions temperatures have risen as high as a record 116° F (48° C). (By comparison, Death Valley, California, has recorded 134° F—56.7° C—which is close to the world record of 136° F—58° C—recorded in Al Aziziyah, Libya, near Tripoli, in 1922). Since the intense heat is accompanied by high humidity, Bahrain can be one of the most uncomfortable spots on Earth. To add to the country's summer misery, a hot, dry, northwesterly wind, known locally as the "summer *shamal*," occasionally brings huge clouds of choking dust from nearby Saudi Arabia and Iran. And from the southwest a hot, dry wind known regionally as the "*gaws*" occasionally brings sky-blackening sandstorms. These storms originate in the deserts of Saudi Arabia and can bury Bahrain beneath a blanket of powdery dust.

Winter brings more moderate temperatures and greater changes in day-to-day weather. From November to March the temperature ranges from 50 to 70° F (10 to 21° C).

Unfortunately, the humidity often rises above 90 percent in the winter. Even though the lower sun season is milder, it is still quite sticky. From December to March, prevailing winds from the southeast, called the "winter *shamal*," bring damp air over the islands. Because Bahrain is surrounded by sea, both seasonal and daily temperatures are fairly uniform. Although average temperatures are quite high, the country lacks the extremes—either high or low—experienced by its mainland neighbors.

Bahrain receives very little precipitation. Average annual rainfall is just 3 to 4 inches (75 to 100 millimeters), nearly all of which falls during the winter months. On average, rain falls only about seven to nine days a year. Evaporation throughout the country greatly exceeds precipitation, resulting in a moisture deficit. During winter months, rains fall in short, though often heavy, storms. After a rain, the *wadis* can become churning torrents of treacherous floodwater. These events, called flash floods in the American desert region, can damage land, roads, and life. Because of the rapid runoff, very little of the water in these streambeds is contained and used for drinking, irrigation, or other useful purposes.

Plant and Animal Life

Bahrain's harsh desert conditions create a difficult and challenging environment for a wide variety of plants and animals. Yet the country is famed for its lush greenery in the middle of the dry desert. Most natural plants are both *halophytic* (salt tolerant) and *xerophytic* (drought resistant). Flowering desert shrubs add color to the dry landscape, and a variety of palm trees grow abundantly. Bahrain has a single quite famous tree called the "Tree of Life"—it stands as a lone sentinel in the desert about 1.2 miles (2 kilometers) from the Jebal al Dukhan. No one can explain its source of water, but travelers marvel at its presence and find its shade a welcome relief from the intense sun.

Plant life in Bahrain is beginning to suffer from increasing salinity (saltiness) of the soil. As more and more fresh water is withdrawn from wells or springs, it is replaced by salt water that seeps into the aquifers (underground deposits of water) from the Persian Gulf, so the groundwater keeps getting saltier and saltier. Some parts of Bahrain are still lushly covered with date palms and other trees, but this is beginning to change. Increasing salinity of ground water, combined with excessive cutting of trees for fuel and other uses, has caused some parts of Bahrain to lose their palm trees altogether.

Bahrain is well known by bird-watchers for its number and great variety of birds. Its mixture of desert, marsh, mudflats, mangrove swamps, and sub-tropical gardens make this island a bird lover's paradise. Shore species such as sandpipers, curlews, herons, and plovers are just a few of the birds that thrive in the extensive low-water mudflats. Mangrove swamps are smelly and polluted but are home to flocks of herons, flamingos, egrets, terns, and gulls, among many other species.

The warm, shallow gulf waters surrounding Bahrain are

habitat for an amazing abundance of sea life. Groupers, mackerels, shrimps, pearl oysters, and dugongs (sea cows, similar to the manatees that live in many Florida streams) flourish in the surrounding gulf. On land, scorpions, snakes, and other reptiles thrive in the hot, dry conditions so prevalent in Bahrain. The gulf region is home to 23 venomous snakes, including the asp, a deadly horned viper. A few hedgehogs, hares, and gazelles can be seen, but you would need to visit the Al-Areen Wildlife Sanctuary to see most animals. Even the camel, the famous "ship of the desert," is rarely seen today in Bahrain. In fact, the durable domesticated donkey is the animal most widely found in Bahrain.

Water

The gulf itself is Bahrain's most important water feature. From the dawn of human settlement to the present day, the sea has been a primary influence on the physical, cultural, and historical geography of this insular (island) nation. Unfortunately, this vital resource—particularly for a country increasingly dependent on tourism as a mainstay of its economy—is being heavily polluted. Oil spills from large tankers, oil refineries, and other sources have damaged coastlines, coral reefs, and sea vegetation.

What do the Bahrainis do for water in this parched land? The country has no fresh surface water—there are no rivers, lakes, or streams anywhere on the islands. Some water is available from the many natural springs found in northern part of the island of Bahrain and on several adjacent islands— these springs have drawn settlers to the islands for centuries— but Bahrainis are worried because water from the springs is becoming increasingly salty. They also are beginning to show the effects of pollution from the country's metal and other industries. To compensate for this loss, Bahrain began building water desalinization plants in the early 1980s. Today, about 60 percent of the country's water supply comes from this source.

The warm, shallow waters surrounding Bahrain are home to a wide variety of sea life. Shrimp fishing has become so popular that it threatens the region's shrimp population. A temporary ban on catching shrimp is aimed at helping replenish supplies.

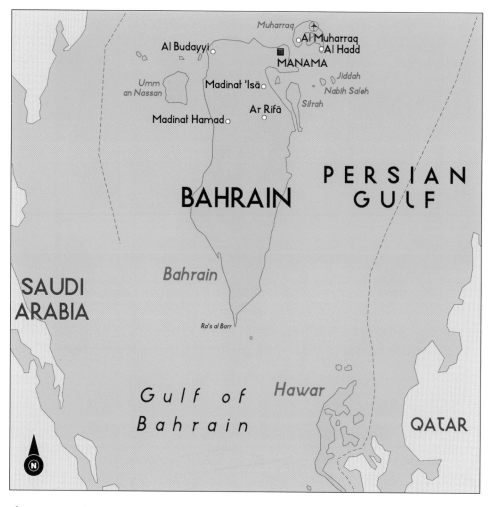

The two most important islands of the 33 that comprise the country of Bahrain are Bahrain and Al Muharraq. These two islands are connected by a causeway that was built in 1929, but there are a number of causeways linking Bahrain's islands and its neighboring countries. Bahrain is only 15 miles from Saudi Arabia and 17 miles from Qatar.

The plants remove salt from seawater, making it suitable for human, industrial, and agricultural use. The desalinization process is much more expensive than obtaining water from springs, but people living in this parched land must have water to survive, so they are willing to pay the price.

In summarizing the importance of the natural landscape to the country and people of Bahrain, several important features stand out:

- The country is small and fragmented into 33 "pieces."

- Through time, Bahrain has been able to take advantage of its location in becoming an early center of trade between the East and West.

- Its springs provided precious fresh water that created a marvelous oasis in the midst of the desert.

- Pearls from the seabed brought wealth to Bahrain for thousands of years.

- For the past century, oil resources (discussed elsewhere in the book) have been a major factor in the region's economic and political climate.

- No larger than many American cities, this parched, sandy, extremely hot country is home to nearly 700,000 people—giving it one of the highest population densities on Earth.

As is true in nearly all the world's major nations, the country's physical environment plays a very important role in influencing the well-being of a nation and its people.

Much can be learned about Bahrain's ancient history from its archaeological sites. Remnants of the once powerful Dilmun empire show a life rich in trade, farming, and art.

3

Bahrain Through Time

As early as 3000 B.C., Bahrain was the center of one of the great trading empires of the ancient world. This legendary empire was called Dilmun, regarded by the Sumerians of Mesopotamia (Iraq) as being the "Land of Immortality." In fact, the Sumerians venerated Dilmun in their poetry, referring to it alternatively as the "Land of Paradise," "Land of the Living," and "Home of the Gods." It has been suggested that the hero-king of the great *Epic of Gilgamesh* traveled to Dilmun in search of the survivors of the Great Flood.

Dilmun—Center of Trade, Commerce, and Conflict

The ancient empire of Dilmun covered most of eastern Arabia and present-day Bahrain. It was based in a land with abundant supplies of fresh spring water. One of the world's first irrigation systems turned the desert into a fertile farming oasis. From these agricultural beginnings, Dilmun developed rapidly into a great center of culture and civilization, as well. Four thousand years ago, as today, this land successfully took advantage of its strategic geographical location. It became an important trade center located between flourishing empires in Mesopotamia to the west and the Indus River Valley to the east (in present-day Pakistan). During the third and second millennia B.C., the merchants of Dilmun transported and traded a wide variety of goods, including spices, silk, and gems, between the lands to the east and west.

Dilmun also produced two of its own exports, items that have been associated with the Persian Gulf region ever since. Dates, from the region's abundant date-palm groves, were and continue to be an important export of Bahrain. Dates are very nutritious—but of greater importance, they dry well and can be preserved for long periods of time. Also, beautiful, luminous pearls—called "fisheyes" in the ancient texts—have been gathered from the surrounding Persian Gulf waters for thousands of years.

Because Dilmun's success was closely tied to trade and commerce between Mesopotamia and the Indus Valley, the empire was largely dependent on the continuing strength of these two regions. It began to decline as a great trade center after the fall of the Indus Valley civilization in the mid-second millennium B.C. Once the great Indus Valley civilization fell, Dilmun could no longer serve as an *entrepôt*, or vital link in trade, between rich markets to the east and west. Eventually, in the 8th century B.C., a much-weakened Dilmun became part of the Assyrian Empire. By 600 B.C., it was integrated into the Babylonian Empire.

Greek and Persian Influence

Little is known about the two centuries falling between Dilmun's occupation by Babylon and the dawn of Greek

Dates have been harvested from Bahrain's plentiful palm groves for centuries. A valuable food and export crop, dates continue to provide a delicacy for which the Persian Gulf is well known.

influence on the region. It is known that Nearchus, a Greek general in the army of Alexander the Great, built a colony on the island of Falaika (off the coast of Kuwait) in the 4th century B.C. From this time until the arrival of Islam in the 7th century A.D., Bahrain fell under the influence of Greek culture. During this long period of nearly a millennium, Bahrain was known by its Greek name, Tylos.

During a period extending from about 300 B.C. to roughly 300 A.D., the residents of Tylos prospered. Pliny, an ancient Roman historian, wrote about Tylos's reputation for beautiful pearls. During this period of approximately 600 years, Bahrain was under the political rule of various Persian empires.

During the 3rd and 4th centuries A.D., many Bahrainis adopted Christianity. Nestorians (a branch of Christianity) became established in Bahrain by the early 5th century. Church records tell us that Bahrain was the seat of two of the five Nestorian bishoprics (administrative regions) existing on the Arabian side of the gulf at the time Islam arrived in the 7th century.

The Bahrainis are very proud that they were one of the first people outside mainland Arabia to accept Islam and to do so peacefully. The prophet Mohammed wrote to the ruler of Bahrain in 640 A.D. and invited him to accept Islam. He did adopt the religion, and for the next two centuries Christians and Muslims lived together peacefully. (Today there is still a tiny group of Bahrainis who practice Christianity.) It was Arab-Muslim geographers of this era who renamed Dilmun, calling it Bahrain. The word *Bahrain* (pronounced bah-rain) is Arabic and means "two seas." The country prospered during the following centuries of Islamic rule. Pearl gathering was the greatest source of wealth. By the 14th century tiny Bahrain had 300 villages. The country's merchants grew rich from profits obtained from the enormous shiny, high-quality pearls. Pearl merchants and sea captains built huge palaces on the island of Bahrain and others in the archipelago.

Bahrain was a part of several Persian empires during the 9th to 11th centuries. One Persian influence was the introduction of Shi'a (a branch of Islam), which rapidly became the dominant faith. The country was also well governed during this period, a condition that helped Bahrain become prosperous once again. This time the country became an important port on the trade routes linking India and Iraq. During the ensuing Middle Ages, Bahrain changed hands often as Sheikhs, or Arab tribal chieftains, bickered and fought constantly with one another over this and other territories.

The Portuguese in Bahrain

Portuguese explorers were the first western Europeans to arrive in Bahrain. They wanted to protect their monopoly over the spice trade that linked Europe with the Spice Islands in the East Indies. By 1521 the Portuguese had seized Bahrain and built a series of fortresses along the Arabian coast. This was a new experience for the countries of the Persian Gulf. For the first time in their history, an outside power was in charge of the region—a position that various foreign powers would hold for some 300 years. Portuguese domination of the gulf reached its peak during the second half of the 16th century. During this time they were in total command of the important spice and silk routes to the Orient. While under foreign control, Bahrain became the most important place on the Arabian coast.

Maintaining control was not an easy task for the Europeans. The Portuguese were constantly challenged by local forces anxious to regain their lost territory. In 1602 local traders successfully rose against the Portuguese and drove them from the islands. The Bahrainis, however, realizing they were no match against the powerful Europeans, turned to Persia for protection. The Shah agreed, and

Seeking to protect their monopoly over the eastern spice trade, the
Portuguese seized control of Bahrain in 1521, building large fortresses to
protect their economic interests. Although the Portuguese were driven
out by a local uprising in 1602, the ruins of this imposing fort remain.

Bahrain once again fell under control of Persia (today's Iran), an arrangement that lasted until the mid-18th century.

Beginning of the Al-Khalifa Dynasty

By the 1700s Bahrain had regained some of its importance as a commercial center, a role that it had enjoyed off and on for the past 4,000 years. Its greatest attractions were beautiful pearls and the islands' freshwater springs. The *oases* (places in a desert where fresh water is available) made possible a relatively productive and somewhat prosperous agricultural community. It had been a part of the Persian Empire for nearly two centuries. But the winds of change were once more blowing over the Persian Gulf and this small group of islands tucked away along its western shore.

Persian rule over Bahrain was broken in 1783 by a powerful clan (extended family) leader, Sheikh Ahmed Al-Fatih, known as "the Conqueror." Persians were driven from their fortress and the Al-Khalifa family began its rule of Bahrain that continues unbroken to the present day. The Al-Khalifas belong to the same clan as the Al-Sabahs, the rulers of Kuwait, and are also distantly related to the Saudi Arabian royal family. The clan belonged to the nomadic Utub, a powerful Bedouin tribe that moved from the interior Arabian Peninsula and settled on the Persian Gulf coast during the 18th century. After wandering eastward to Qatar and northward to Kuwait, the family returned to settle and establish a pearling center at Zubara in present-day Qatar. Soon, however, their attention turned to the tempting springs and lush green oases just across the water in Bahrain.

Persia was in control of Bahrain at the time, but Ahmad ibu Muhammad, the first Al-Khalifa ruler, captured Bahrain from the hands of the Persians. As the newly established ruler, Muhammad introduced policies that enabled Bahrain's ports to once again develop into prosperous trade and pearling centers. However, the Al-Khalifa family followed—

and still follows—the Sunni branch of Islam, whereas the Bahrainis had always been Shi'a Muslims. Repercussions from this conquest and its accompanying religious differences continue to plague the island nation today, more than two centuries later.

British Control of Bahrain

Bahrain, along with other Persian Gulf countries, came under British influence during the early 19th century. The gulf region had become extremely important to the British; India was now a British colony, and Britain was anxious to protect the sea routes that linked the two lands. But the Persian Gulf region was troubled. Pirates constantly sacked ships, and in Bahrain there was constant feuding among the Al-Khalifa family members who were heirs to power. The British became convinced that they needed to get involved to help keep order. In 1820 Bahrain and several other countries in the region signed a "General Treaty of Peace," which was an attempt to stop the ongoing political conflicts and make the seas safe from piracy. This was the first of many treaties signed with Britain, creating an alliance that would exist until Bahrain's independence in 1971.

Despite the treaty, between 1820 and 1869 Bahrain seemed to be in constant turmoil as Al-Khalifa family members continued to feud. Rival factions fought one another for control of the government, and there were many assassinations. By 1869 the British had tired of the constant conflict and stepped in to stop it. Feuding leaders and rivals were removed not only from power but from the country, as well. Bahrain was made a British protectorate, and the country's government was placed in the hands of 21-year-old Al-Khalifa family member Sheikh Isa ibn Ali Al-Khalifa.

Bahrain's young new ruler signed an agreement making Britain responsible for Bahrain's defense and foreign policy. The search for petroleum had begun in the Middle East. In return for British protection, Sheikh Isa agreed not to give any concessions for oil exploration without British approval. The agreement was important because the British were already developing oil fields in Iran. It also gave the British a very strong position in the unfolding economics and politics that would grow around the discovery and production of the region's petroleum resources.

By the 1880s Britain began to regard Bahrain and the Persian Gulf region as its own private reserve. When the Ottoman Empire threatened to establish a presence in Bahrain, Britain immediately forced an agreement from the Sheikh that neither he nor his heirs or successors would enter into negotiations of any kind with any country other than Britain without British approval. Soon other countries in the region were also pressured into agreeing to these conditions. Among other restrictions, this meant that none of the small countries bordering the western coast of the gulf could allow any of their territory to be owned or controlled in any way by any country other than Britain. In essence, these agreements gave Great Britain a free hand in using the region to support its own interests—including military control and oil exploration and development.

Bahrain Becomes Isolated

The impact of the treaty with Britain was that Bahrain and the other gulf states became isolated from the rest of the world. Britain guarded them jealously to keep other European countries from entering the region. The Persian Gulf became a great British "lake," and Britain maintained it as such. Most of the gulf countries, including Bahrain, had no recognized legal status within the British Empire. They were simply described as being "in treaty relationships" with Britain—it was almost as if they were prisoners, with little freedom and few rights or powers of their own.

The British-imposed isolation caused Bahrain and the

other gulf countries to become very inward looking and traditional—which is to say, slow to change. Until oil was discovered, Bahrain and the gulf states were like places where time had stood still. Bahrainis seldom ventured outside the Persian Gulf area, other than perhaps an occasional trip to Bombay (Mumbai), a large city in the British colony of India. Until recently, Bahrain's ties to India have been fairly strong. For example, the Indian rupee, their monetary unit, was also the major Bahraini currency, particularly in coastal communities. And until the 1940s Indian stamps were marked over with "Bahrain" and "Kuwait."

Some good—at least as judged by local standards—came from the isolation. The fact that Bahrain was a backwater gave it a kind of protection from outside cultural influences. People were able to preserve their social, economic, and political systems as well as other aspects of their way of life. They also were able to continue living by traditional Arab tribal customs. Even after oil was discovered, they remained relatively isolated and were able to hold on to many of their cultural traditions. Neither Bahrain nor any other gulf state, however, could act in an official capacity with any other country. The British conducted all foreign relations on their behalf. Also, all movement into or out of Bahrain and the gulf region was subject to British permission. All of this was accomplished by a very small group of four or five British officers who managed to protect British interests and keep the Persian Gulf a peaceful body of water.

An interesting story highlights this bit of British history in the gulf. In 1934 the political agent in Bahrain received a telegram from the British consul in Basra, Iraq, informing him that he had granted an entry visa to Bahrain to a Mr. Harding of American Express. The agent panicked when he read the telegram. He did not want any Americans in Bahrain. He therefore decided to block Mr. Harding's entry. The agent went to the airport and prepared to send him back immediately after his plane landed. However, to his great surprise and relief, Mr. Harding turned out to be an Englishman, and he was allowed into Bahrain.

Unfortunately, Britain's official policy against interference in Bahrain and the other gulf states also meant that British officials did not try to introduce any much-needed social and economic reforms. Representatives of the British government did not introduce schools, hospitals, or public services of any kind. This just served to increase the isolation of the region. By the same token, this British relationship protected Bahrain's political and territorial integrity, which was especially important during the 1920s and 1930s when Saudi Arabia, Iran, and Iraq entered the political arena as growing regional powers. The charismatic leaders of all three countries laid claim to various parts of the gulf region. It took an enormous diplomatic effort, but Britain was successful in resisting these clams and maintaining the region's political status quo.

The continuing isolation of Bahrain and the other gulf states served to strengthen the respective positions of the region's different rulers. As long as they fulfilled their treaty obligations, Britain left all local decisions up to them and did not interfere in domestic matters. Their treaty obligations were largely concerned with the absence of foreign relations and the avoidance of any sort of hostilities at sea. Under this arrangement, the rulers gained more power and prestige.

The fact that Britain interacted on an individual basis with each country served to keep the states from needing to interact with one another. This further encouraged feelings of separation between the countries. For example, the treaty stated that every ship had to fly the flag of the state to which it belonged. In time, each state became identified with a flag. The daily identification of the individual states with its own flag by each seafaring population increased feelings of separation. Although a flag and a passport are only symbols of a state, their repeated use brings about a sense of national identity. Bahrain and Oman even adopted national anthems by the 1930s. The other gulf states also soon adopted anthems. This process of states becoming increasingly separate, viable, self-contained political entities accelerated as the British presence continued.

For a time all went well for Bahrain. Then trouble brewed as the ruler of Iran, Shah Reza Pahlavi, continued his country's long-standing claim to Bahrain. He insisted that Bahrain was part of his "natural empire." The shah based his ownership claims on Iran's 16th-century occupation of Bahrain. He also suggested that Bahrain was part of Iran because a large number of Bahrainis were descended from Iranian immigrants. The British managed to persuade Iran to renounce its claim, and the United Nations recommended that Bahrain should become an independent state. The shah accepted the resolution and made no further claims on Bahrain. But on the eve of independence, an empty desk marked "Province of Bahrain" stood in the Iranian capitol.

Oil Brings Change

Oil had been used in the region for thousands of year. Sailors used the dark goo that oozed up from the sands to caulk the hulls of their wooden *dhows* (sailboats). By the 19th century, oil was becoming increasingly important, as grease and fuel were needed for the machines that powered the Industrial Revolution. Soon petroleum-based kerosene would become a major source of lamplight. Oil suddenly became a precious and much-sought-after resource. Its importance was to have a huge impact on the future and fortunes of the Persian Gulf countries and the entire Middle East.

The British government of India controlled all the original oil rights (called *concessions*) in the Persian Gulf region. The rulers of Bahrain and other Persian Gulf countries granted oil concession leases—agreements with

The industrial age brought new importance to Bahrain's underground oil. Demand for petroleum products has dramatically increased since the first wells were drilled in 1932, which has vastly increased the nation's wealth.

specific terms and conditions—separately to companies. These agreements ultimately determined where drilling occurred, by whom, and who benefited. Oil was discovered and production began in Bahrain in 1932. With oil royalties gushing in, the country's economy flourished while other gulf countries suffered severe economic problems associated with the global depression.

Oil played an important role in the political geography of the Gulf region. Before petroleum became an important resource and source of great wealth, the area did not have formally established political boundaries. There had been no need to define borders. "Owned" territory was a foreign concept to people who were governed by the so-called Law of the Desert, often defined as "Who has the power has the territory!" Broad transitional zones rather than established "boundary lines" defined territories. The oil concessions created a new question of territorial ownership. With legally binding claims and billions of dollars in oil money at stake, both landowners and oil companies needed to know the exact location and extent of their claims. How could this be done when there were no boundary lines between countries?

On the mainland of the Arabian Peninsula, not having boundaries posed a serious challenge. Fortunately for Bahrain, its insular status did not present any problems in this regard. However, territorial disputes between a number of states facing the gulf began soon after the first signing of oil concessions. Even Bahrain has been involved in these arguments. For example, it has quarreled with Qatar over Zubarah (on Qatar's west coast) and the Hawar Islands lying between them. Even though the oil leases were signed in the 1930s, problems continue today between Bahrain and Qatar over the tiny islet of Fasht al-Dibal, one of the Hawar Islands.

Opening the region to the outside world was one of the most striking changes brought about by the oil companies. The British could no longer restrict and control the entrance of foreigners to Bahrain and the other gulf states. Geologists, refinery workers, managers, and other petroleum workers began to come to Bahrain and the other areas bordering the Persian Gulf in increasing numbers. The old days of being a backwater ended. In the late 1920s the first American oil concession in the gulf region was obtained in Bahrain by the Standard Oil Company of California (SoCal). The British government, however, objected vigorously to the entry of an American company in the region. But Britain finally accepted the concession on condition that the company holding the Bahrain concession would be British. SoCal helped form the Bahrain Petroleum Company (BAPCO), a "British" company registered in Canada, with one of its five directors being British. BAPCO began drilling for oil in Bahrain in the fall of 1931. In the summer of 1932, at a depth of just over 2,000 feet (210 meters), oil was struck and production began. A year later, SoCal obtained a concession from Saudi Arabia, resulting in the formation of ARAMCO (the Arabian-American [Oil] Company). With this venture, American oil companies had become firmly established in the Persian Gulf region.

Before the arrival of the oil companies in the gulf, local rulers generally had been passive in their relationships with Britain. As long as they upheld their end of the treaties, they had little contact with the British officials, except in matters of ceremony. But once negotiations for oil concessions began, the situation changed. The ruler of Bahrain, for example, was permitted to participate in the discussions. His signature was required for the business at hand to be finalized. He was aware of the economic benefits and could drive a hard bargain by holding out for the best financial terms possible. A ruler was personally responsible to Britain for the actions of his people. Any infringement of the treaty regulations invoked the anger of the British.

Bahrain's economic activities provided its rulers and their families with their main sources of income. The pearling industry had been vital to the country's pre-oil economy. However, pearling suffered a devastating collapse after America's Wall Street stock market crash of 1929.

During the global economic depression that followed, there was a much lower demand for costly luxury items such as pearls. Japan's introduction of cultured (artificially grown) pearls into the global market brought further decline to Bahrain's economy. Oil companies, seeking concessions during the 1930s, saved Bahrain and other gulf countries from sure financial ruin.

Oil concessions offered two very important things to Bahrain and the other oil-producing states in the region. First, they helped bring relief from extreme poverty. Second, they brought about a subtle and important change in the relationship between a ruler and his people. The oil agreements provided rulers with monthly fees. Even though these monthly payments were very small, they allowed the rulers for the first time to be financially independent of their people. This allowed the rulers to become generous to their people without taxation. Rulers were the major recipients of oil income. Typically, rulers distributed large sums of money to various developmental projects.

The government of Bahrain used much of the oil revenues to create new departments. The extra investment helped the educational system to expand. For example, in 1930 there were 500 students enrolled in Bahrain's educational system, but by 1938 the number had tripled. In addition, the country installed a printing press in 1937, and the gulf's first movie theater opened in 1939. Many social and cultural clubs were formed. BAPCO began filling vacant positions in its oil company, thereby providing much-needed jobs to those who had been left unemployed as a result of the cutbacks in the pearling industry.

With oil wealth flowing into the country, government began to change. Departments were set up, and councils of ministers were appointed. Secretaries were employed, and salary scales were drawn up. These additional layers of government helped to further separate rulers from their people. Direct access to the ruler became much more difficult. Previously, citizens could approach the ruler about any problem, no matter how personal. Now requests and petitions had to be channeled through an ever-larger bureaucracy. The close tie between a ruler and his people was broken.

Many other changes were occurring in Bahrain. Pearl divers

left their trade to work in the oil fields, where they were joined may many of the country's farmers. Traditional settlement patterns and ways of life began to disappear, as people moved from rural villages to the growing cities where wage-paying jobs could be found. As old problems disappeared, new problems seemed to spring up like dust rising in a desert storm. For example, when American engineers arrived in 1936 to build a new refinery, Bahrain's merchants prospered, and many young men found good jobs in construction. However, the refinery was completed in 1937, and with building jobs and American builders gone, a depression settled on Bahrain. Educated young men were unable to find jobs, and merchants went out of business as a result of the decline in trade. Bahrain's royal family was reaping huge oil revenues, while most Bahrainis watched incomes dwindle—and strong resentments began to grow among the people.

Growing Unrest

In the late 1930s tensions in Bahrain reached a boiling point. The growing bureaucracy had driven a wedge between the people and their ruler. The ruling family was gaining great wealth, while the people were sinking into poverty. Courts of law were inefficient and prejudiced. The educational system was producing graduates who lacked the knowledge and skills needed to work in the oil industry or for the government. Employment at BAPCO discriminated against poorly educated native Bahrainis who in turn deeply resented not being able to work in their own oil refineries.

Outcries were raised against the inefficient police, the passport office, prisons, and many other government functions overseen by the British adviser to the ruler. Various opposition societies were formed, but they could not sustain momentum in the face of opposition from the political agent, Britain's adviser to the ruler, and BAPCO. Eventually, however, some of the reform movement's demands were met, and in 1938 the mounting grievances finally resulted in a reform movement. A national labor committee was formed, and a labor relation's representative to BAPCO was appointed. The government also employed an educational expert to advise Bahrain on how to improve its educational system.

During World War II (1939–1945), both political and social unrest declined. Other than in private conversation, there were few places people could gather and freely complain about the government. Two important developments did occur during this period. *The Bahrain,* the first newspaper to be produced in the Persian Gulf region, was published in 1939. Also, the British Ministry of Information established the Bahrain broadcasting station in 1940. The newspaper appealed to literate Bahrainis—those few who were able to read; radio broadcasts appealed mainly to the largely illiterate Bahrain population. British slogans promoting freedom and democracy became very popular with the people of Bahrain, who sought to grasp the same principles for themselves.

Steps Toward Independence

Following World War II, Bahrain increased efforts to fully free itself from British influence. The United Nations' planned partition of Palestine and the movement toward Arab nationalism were only two of the influential trends that strengthened Bahrainis' desire for freedom. Many of the region's leaders were voicing a desire for the loosening of European control throughout the Arab world. In Bahrain the social clubs and the press continued to be the places where citizens could express their discontent and demands for greater participation. In 1956, the year of the Suez war, open defiance of the government broke out in Bahrain. British forces suppressed all opposition and imposed a state of emergency that lasted for the next 10 years, forbidding all political activity. A council was formed to watch over Bahraini government and affairs. While the council sought to increase political participation of the Bahraini people, it never directly challenged the power or authority of the ruling Al-Khalifa family.

Some forms of representative government already existed in Bahrain at this time. Half of the members of the municipal council were elected, and the government appointed the other half. In addition, women who owned property were entitled to vote. There also were various councils to handle local affairs, such as religious trust funds and matters relating to water and agriculture. However, the ruler of Bahrain continued to operate under his own philosophy: that people would do well to do what they do best. He believed the government should govern, the farmer should farm, the merchant should trade, and the workers should work. The less that people meddled in the role of others, the better Bahrain would function. The British in Bahrain shared the people's desire for more participation in government but were reluctant to do anything that might undermine the ruler.

In 1956 when the British Foreign Secretary visited Bahrain, violence erupted once again. Angry demonstrators denounced Britain's role in Bahrain. They were particularly upset over the British adviser's influence on the ruling family and government of Bahrain. A few days later a dispute in a local market involving a municipal official erupted into violence. Police fired into the crowd, killing and wounding several demonstrators. A general strike against the government was called, and all activity in Bahrain came to a halt. Finally the time for compromise and discussion had arrived in Bahrain.

Parties representing Bahrain and its government met with British officials, and the sides agreed on a number of critical issues. Two particularly important points were agreed on: First, a Committee for National Unity would be formed and recognized by the ruler; second, the controversial office of British adviser to the ruler would be abolished.

During the decade-long period of unrest, the press was strictly controlled, and the police force was strengthened. In March 1965 BAPCO laid off hundreds of workers, and violence once again erupted in the streets of Bahrain. This time students went on strike and were joined by various political groups that had been all but silent for previous decade. They united to form the National Front for Progressive Force and called a general strike. Even though demonstrations and increasing violence conveyed the people's rapidly growing discontent, the government held firm control, and the National Front fizzled out. However, once again events in the Arab world started major change in Bahrain. In 1968 the British announced plans to close all of its bases east of the Suez Canal within three years and withdraw its military and political presence in the Persian Gulf. At the same time Britain was announcing plans to withdraw from Bahrain and other gulf nations, Iran began talking again about its old claims to Bahrain. Suddenly Bahrainis were panic-stricken at the thought of losing British protection.

All of the gulf states were reeling with the news of Britain's imminent departure from the region, alarmed over national security issues in the absence of a British political and military presence. Several gulf states united to form federations for mutual protection. However, Bahrain was opposed to this idea. Although Bahrain had far less wealth than the other gulf states, it had a far more advanced system of government and a more diverse social structure. Bahrain's progressive state of affairs combined with the fact that it had the largest population convinced the country's rulers that it should opt for independence rather than join a federation and play a minor role in its administration.

Bahrain Gains Its Independence

With British influence in decline, the time was ripe for Bahrain to seek independence. In 1970, in response to a

British diplomatic initiative, the shah of Iran agreed to a UN referendum in Bahrain to determine the wishes of the Bahrainis. The results were overwhelmingly in favor of Bahrain's independence. This secret arrangement was made known only after the death of the shah, but was an effective, face-saving way to allow Iran to give up its claims on Bahrain.

Bahrain finally gained full independence in 1971. Before independence, it had been a British protectorate. Following independence, the Al-Khalifa family continued its domination of Bahrain's government and society, something it had done since 1783. Isa bin Salman (a member of the Al-Khalifa family) became the new country's first *emir* (leader). The emir's brothers, sons, cousins, and uncles continued to control all the major decision-making processes in Bahrain. But a constitution was adopted, and the emir promised Bahrain's people the necessary framework for participatory government. Unfortunately the emir's idea of a constitution was more an expression of royal benevolence than a document giving the people the right to participate in government.

National Assembly Formed

In 1972 Sheikh Isa decreed that a constitutional assembly would be set up to discuss and ratify the constitution. The assembly was partly elected and partly appointed by the government. Once the constitution was ratified, elections were held for members of the National Assembly, called for in the constitution. Two main political coalitions emerged from the short-lived National Assembly. The first and largest was the People's Bloc, a group containing socialists, leftists, communists, and other constituents aligned with the workers, students, and intellectual elements of Bahrain. The other group, the Religious Bloc, represented the rural Shi'a and took a religious stance on matters of education, moral conduct, and religious observances.

The assembly only held two sessions. During the second

Bahrain chose Sheikh Isa bin Salman as its first leader after it achieved independence in 1971. Sheikh Isa was a valuable Western ally.

session, huge differences arose between the government and the People's Bloc. One problem area was the security bill. Sheikh Isa had issued a law that permitted the government to arrest and imprison any person suspected of being a threat to national security. The National Assembly saw this bill as an infringement on its authority as the only legislative body in Bahrain. Another bone of contention was an agreement between the government and the United States. The United States received naval and military facilities in exchange for an annual payment of $4 million. The agreement was not secret, but it had not been given widespread publicity. This aroused the suspicions of National Assembly members. The National Assembly was against this agreement because of U.S. support of Israel. The agreement was cancelled in 1977—although the United States continues to maintain contacts with Bahrain.

Sheikh Isa soon dissolved the National Assembly, and it has never been reconvened. The dissolution of the National Assembly occurred shortly before the oil boom and right after the 1973 Arab-Israeli War. The outcome of the 1973 war began a new phase of life for Bahrain and the other gulf states. Suddenly, thanks to their oil, they had clout on the international stage. Vulnerability was replaced by a sense of greater self-confidence. The gulf states negotiated their oil leases very successfully and became rich beyond their wildest dreams. They began major development projects with this newfound wealth, bringing in foreign designers and construction workers to complete them. Unfortunately, most of these projects wasted a huge amount of money and did not turn out as planned.

Iran's Plot Uncovered

By the mid-1970s the shah of Iran emerged as the "policeman" of the Persian Gulf region. In 1975 Iran obtained joint control of the Shatt-al-Arab, the river formed by the joining of the Tigris and Euphrates. However, the shah had lost the support of most Iranians, and in 1979 he was overthrown and replaced by the Islamic Republic of Iran—and with the coup came the revival of Islamic fundamentalism. Tehran urged the Shi'a population of Bahrain to overturn the government. During 1979 Ayatollah Rouhani revived Iran's claim to Bahrain and began talk of annexing it. Iran became a source of inspiration to the discontented Shi'a population of Bahrain.

In 1981 a plot to overthrow the government of Bahrain was uncovered and defused. An immigration officer in Dubai airport noticed some discrepancies in the passports of some young men who were waiting to board a flight for Bahrain. These men were all gulf Arabs with military equipment, supposedly supplied by Iran. Others had received their military training in Iran. The attempted coup led to the discovery of the Islamic Front for the Liberation of Bahrain, with headquarters in Tehran. Seventy-three men were arrested, tried, and imprisoned for this criminal plot. Scared of Iran's growing shadow, Bahrain turned to Saudi Arabia for protection, which resulted in the almost immediate signing of a security pact with its powerful neighbor. It had only been a decade (almost to the day) since Britain had withdrawn from Bahrain, and Saudi Arabia was asked to assume Britain's old protective role.

Saudi Arabia's Friendship

Saudi influence had been strong in Bahrain since Britain had withdrawn. Bahrain did not have any boundary or territorial quarrels with Saudi Arabia, so it was only natural that they turn to them for protection. Bahrain reaped major benefits from a closer relationship with Saudi Arabia. It was successful in establishing an offshore banking sector in 1975. The move was successful and timely because Bahrain was searching for something to replace its dwindling oil reserves. By 1985 there were 74 offshore banks operating out of Bahrain. Also, very significantly, Saudi Arabia gave the banks concessions to operate in Saudi Arabia—giving them a distinct advantage over other banks. Bahrain was rapidly becoming a service center for wealthy Saudi Arabia.

Saudi Arabia has helped Bahrain in other ways, too. The offshore oil field, Abu Safa, which is shared by Saudi Arabia and Bahrain, provides a large part of Bahrain's income, because Saudi Arabia has ensured the production level of the field. In addition, Saudi influence has been very important in attracting a number of Organization of Petroleum Exporting Countries (OPEC)-sponsored projects to Bahrain, one of which is the Gulf University. Also, a causeway was built and opened in 1986, connecting Bahrain and Saudi Arabia. Financed by Saudi Arabia, the causeway served to link the two countries even more closely.

Bahrain has one of the largest blue-collar labor forces in the gulf region. Labor problems have always been an important part of political life in Bahrain. The strikes and labor unrest of 1938 gave rise to a labor committee under the chairmanship of a representative of the ruler. The labor committee's job was to meet with the management of BAPCO on behalf of the workers. A labor law enacted in 1976 allows for mediation by the Ministry of Labor in any dispute and for outstanding matters to go to arbitration before mixed courts. However, strikes are still illegal, and the country has no organized labor unions.

As a counterpart to the large number of blue-collar workers, a growing white-collar workforce has been created by the country's many service companies and financial institutions. During the oil boom period many young men from poor families worked hard to attain technical and medical management positions. Many more Bahrainis became educated than in decades past, and the country began to develop a growing and thriving middle class. However, the recession of the 1980s once again caused Bahrainis to become tense and anxious. Government spending had been reduced, the offshore banking industry was suffering hard times and the Iran-Iraq War revived old tensions. Bahrain's economy was generally depressed with unemployment growing, and

Sheikh Isa bin Salman groomed his son Hamad bin Isa as his successor. After Sheikh Isa's death from a heart attack in 1999, Hamad became leader of Bahrain. The younger Sheikh's more liberal leadership has eased tensions in the country.

young Bahrainis were increasingly discontent with their lack of decision-making ability. Internal discontent was once again reaching the breaking point; since 1980 Bahrain's government has survived at least three coup attempts—all of which were inspired by Iranians.

On March 6, 1999, the ruling emir, Sheikh Isa bin Salman Al-Khalifa, died of natural causes at the age of 65. His son, Sheikh Hamad ibn Isa Al-Khalifa, is the country's current ruler. He appears to be committed to becoming more democratic and to giving the Bahraini people a greater voice in determining policies and planning their country's future. This more liberal approach seems to have eased social tensions considerably in Bahrain.

Bahrain's devotion to Islam is evidenced by the elaborate Al Fateh Mosque, or Grand Mosque. Bahrain's largest mosque, it is capable of accommodating up to 7,000 worshippers and houses the Religious Institute for Islamic Affairs.

4

People and Their Culture

B ahrain's roughly 700,000 people represent a varied mix of cultures and national origins. Even so, its population is one of the most homogeneous in the region. In fact, nearly two of every three of the country's citizens belongs to the dominant ethnic group, the Bahraini—early settlers from whom the country and its largest island take their name. The various ethnic groups live in communities scattered about the large island of Bahrain and on several of the other islands in the chain. Traditionally, there was very little intermingling among groups sharing different ways of life. Today this practice of cultural isolation is breaking down—particularly in the cities of Manama and Muharraq, where people of all races and cultures mingle in schools, market-places, and workplaces.

    One of the most significant cultural differences, and one that has caused some conflict over the years, is religion. The original people of the islands, the Baharinah, are Shi'a Muslims. The remainder of the native population, those who came to the islands with the ruling Al-Khalifa family in the 18th century, are Sunni Muslims. The exact proportions of the two Muslim sects are not known, but it is generally believed that the Shi'a constitute more than two-thirds of the population. In this chapter, you will learn more about Bahrain's people, including their population, settlement, and important aspects of their way of life.

Population

The exact population of Bahrain is not known. Most reliable estimates place the number at between 650,000 and 700,000. This figure is staggering for such a small country, only the size of many U.S. counties, most of which is unsettled desert. For the country as a whole, the population density would be up to 2,700 people per square mile (1,025 per square kilometer). But in this parched land, most people are clustered into a very small portion of the total area, making the actual density much higher in settled areas.

There are many other ways to view a country's population. For example, nearly 40 percent of Bahrain's people are under 20 years old. These young people soon will be reaching an age at which they will want to begin their own families. With a current annual rate of natural increase (RNI) of an estimated 1.7 to 1.9 percent, this means that the country's population is going to continue growing at a faster rate than the annual world average of 1.3 percent. Another way people can be counted is by gender. Nearly 60 percent of Bahrain's population is male; 40 percent, female. Few countries in the world can match this imbalance of the sexes. The high number of foreign residents who have come to Bahrain to work in the country's industries explains the difference. About 75 percent of these foreign residents are male. The male-to-female ratio among native Bahrainis is more balanced, being nearly equal with males only slightly outnumbering females.

Life expectancy is another way to view a population. This figure is an important indicator of many other conditions, including diet, hygiene, health care, educational level, and environmental quality. For the average Bahrain citizen, the news is very good. Men in can expect to live an average of 73 years and women an average of 78. This compares to a world average of only 65 and 69, respectively. These figures speak very well of the quality of life in Bahrain.

Who Are the Bahraini People?

Bahrainis make up nearly two-thirds of the country's population. The second largest group, numbering about 19 percent of the population, is made up of a mixture of southern and eastern Asiatic people, most of whom came to Bahrain during recent decades to work in various industries. Finally, because of the longstanding historical links with the Persian Empire (Iran), about 8 percent of the country's people trace their origins to that region of the world. The remaining 3 percent of the population has come from various parts of the world, including Western nations, the majority from Britain

Nearly a third of Bahrain's population is composed of foreign workers—an estimated 230,000 of them. The petroleum industry in particular has created more jobs than local people can fill, so as is true of most other Persian Gulf states, workers from various countries have flocked to Bahrain to fill the vacant positions. They have come from India, Iran, Pakistan, East Asia, Europe, the United States, and elsewhere. Even with this huge influx of international workers, Bahrain is one of the few countries in the gulf region in which its own citizens remain in the majority.

The largest single foreign community is Indian. It grew

Nearly one-third of Bahrain's population is composed of foreign workers, many of whom are from India. Pressure to fill white-collar jobs gave educated Indian immigrants an edge over less educated Bahrainis. To ease tensions, Bahrain has undertaken an aggressive campaign to find jobs for its citizens.

over the years as a result of close links between Bahrain and India, including a long trading relationship. There were not enough educated Bahrainis to fill the many white-collar positions when oil companies first came to Bahrain in the 1930s, so many of these jobs went to better-educated Indians. Many native people deeply resented the Indians, however, because as British citizens they received special privileges and treatment.

Iranians comprise another sizeable group of foreign residents. They usually live in cities and hold merchants' positions in the economy. Some Iranian families have been in the country for centuries. Others arrived during the 1920s and 1930s to escape Iran's high taxes. Although like the majority of Bahrainis these

Iranians are Shi'a Muslims, they are separate from the native Baharinah, with whom they do not necessarily culturally identify.

Rural and Urban Living

Bahrain's original inhabitants, the Baharinah, were nomadic, and traditionally they have continued to be a rural people. Because of the country's very small size, however, even the earliest settlers had to give up their nomadic way of living. Settlements became permanent. Many of the villages and towns of Bahrain were established centuries ago near oases formed by natural springs, wells, or water deposits beneath dry riverbeds.

Many of the Baharinah, after settling in Bahrain and giving up their nomadic life, began to work in agriculture—particularly in association with the date-palm industry. Some of them have moved to towns and become prominent merchants. The Al Urayidh family is one such family. Some of its members are prominent in the government today. When the Bahrain Petroleum Company (BAPCO) started operations in the 1930s, many Baharinah became oil-field workers and migrated to the main towns. The introduction of widespread educational facilities also provided the Baharinah with the means to acquire new skills and move away from their traditional occupations. Despite their rural to urban migration over the years, one of their most important cultural and political activities has remained their congregation in the *ma'tam*, a funeral house where the *Ashura* (the commemoration of the Imam Husain's martyrdom) is observed. To the Shi'a, the *ta'ziyah*, which is part of Ashura celebrations, and the *ma'tuam*, in which rituals and missionary works are held, symbolize the rejection of worldly power and the forms of government with which it is associated. Such fundamentalism is at the root of much Middle Eastern political unrest that today is directed toward the West.

Most of Bahrain's people live in cities or suburbs. Many men of working age commute from the villages where they live to the urban areas where they work. The capital and largest city, Manama, is the chief commercial and cultural center of Bahrain. In 2001 its estimated population slightly exceeded 200,000. In 1960 Bahrain began to diversify its industry from simple oil production into petroleum refining, petrochemicals, aluminum production, and service-oriented industries such as banking and finance. When this occurred, the population of Manama exploded. Entire villages, fields, and palm and fruit groves became incorporated into the city, resulting in the occurrence of urban sprawl—Persian Gulf style. As the city continued to swell in area, land began to be reclaimed from the sea. Hundreds of hectares (a hectare is an area equivalent to 2.47 acres) of land were drained or filled in to create dry land for building and settlement expansion.

The old sections of Manama contain the traditional brick houses with their central courtyards and wind towers reminiscent of southern Iran. Covered *bazaars* (marketplaces) are also found in the older urban areas of the city. In the newer and less crowded neighborhoods, multistory apartment complexes, high-rise hotels and office buildings, and supermarkets replace the more traditional urban structures. Because most of Bahrain's foreign workers tend to live in the city, Manama has a cosmopolitan atmosphere and is always bustling with activity and tempting smells.

The second-largest and only other major city in Bahrain is Al Muharraq. Until the 1930s the ruler lived in Al Muharraq, and for over a century the city served as the country's center of government. During the mid-20th century, after the ruling al Khalifa moved his family to the island of Bahrain, the city of Al Muharraq stagnated. During the 1970s, however, a $60 million U.S. shipbuilding and repair yard was built near the small fishing village of Al Hadd. The construction of this facility helped to stimulate an investment and development boom in Al Muharraq.

The other main towns of Bahrain are Jidd Hafs, Ar-Rifā

Other than Manama, Al Muharraq is the only other major city in Bahrain. Arad Fort was built by the Portuguese in the 17th century and is located near the strategic waterways between Bahrain Island and Al Muharraq.

Sitrah, and Madinat 'Isá. Jidd Hafs was a fairly prosperous village of date palm groves during the 19th and early 20th centuries. The village produced medicines and drugs made from the buds, flowers, and pollen of palm trees. However, by 1975 Jidd Hafs had been absorbed into the rapidly expanding Manama as its biggest suburb. Ar Rifā ash Sharqi and Ar-Rifā al

Gharbi were established in the 19th century in the central region of Bahrain, both being located close to natural springs. They grew rapidly after 1952 when Sheikh Salman ibn Hamad Al-Khalifa established his official residence there. Ar Rifāʾs importance as Bahrain's political center continued under Sheikh Isa ibn Salman Al-Khalifa, who built his palace in the town. Several members of his family also built residences in the community. The town of Sitrah was once a center of date-palm-cultivating villages, but since 1970 a residential housing boom fused the villages into one huge suburban town. Madinat ʾIsá was a planned community built to relieve the congestion in Manama and some of the closer suburbs such as Jidd Hafs and Sanabis.

Away from the major cities, a few small villages continue to survive where the population still lives from traditional agriculture. Traveling only 20 minutes from the tinted glass and polished marble of Manama and its suburbs, one reaches another world. The arrival of electricity is perhaps *the* major change that has come to these rural villages over the past 200 years. The contrast is even more evident when one observes that these scattered rural villages are often interspersed with new housing developments that are often inhabited by foreigners. The southern half of the island of Bahrain has few people and no communities of any size or importance.

Religion and Language

Islam is the state religion of Bahrain, and 85 percent of the population is Muslim. The majority of Muslims (70 percent) are members of the *Shiʾa* (Shiʾite) sect or group, while the remainder are *Sunni*. The religious structure of Bahrain, with a Shiʾa majority, is unique in the Persian Gulf region because the ruling family belongs to the Sunni branch of Islam. Since Sunni Muslims hold the reigns of political and economic power in the country, they also are the most powerful and wealthy of the country's people. This leaves the Shiʾa majority as the poorer and less empowered element of society—a situation that continues to create considerable ill feeling and conflict in Bahrain.

The Sunni community is composed of three main groups. The first group includes the tribes who accompanied the Al-Khalifa family to Bahrain in 1783: the Al Rumahi, Al Musallam, Sudan, and Al Dowasir tribes. This closely knit group formed the backbone of Bahrain's defense force for many years. After Britain took over responsibility for the country's defense, this group of Sunnis turned to organizing the pearling fleets and occasionally worked as divers. As a rule they did not engage in agriculture or trade, but once the pearling industry collapsed, they rather reluctantly became affiliated with the oil industry and certain forms of trade.

A second group of Sunnis are the *Nejdis*. They left their homes in Nejd, a region in central Arabia surrounding present-day Riyadh, to settle in Bahrain at the same time as the Al-Khalifa family. They are, however, nontribal. Some of the well-known Nejdi families of Bahrain are the Al Qusaibi and the Al Zayyani. They are urban, and most of them are actively engaged in trade and commerce. Several of the men serve as senior government officials.

The third, and last, group of Sunnis in Bahrain is the *Hawala*. The word Hawala is said to have derived from the Arabic verb *tahawwalah* (to change). In the gulf region, the term applies to those Arabs who once had emigrated to Persia (Iran) and then the Arab coast. The Hawala people of Bahrain traditionally have been engaged in commerce and trade. Together with the Nejdis, they constitute a community similar to that of the merchant notables in nearby Kuwait. Their names are well-known today. The merchant family of Kanoo runs the Yusif bin Ahmad Kanoo companies, the largest shipping and airline agents in the Arabian Peninsula. The Fakhro family is another Hawala family of importance and stature in Bahrain. The minister of Education, Dr. Ali Fakhro, is a member of this family. The Shirawi family also claims an important government member, Yusif Shirawi, the current minister of Industry and Development for Bahrain.

When the ancestors of the present rulers, the Al-Khalifa family and their followers, arrived in Bahrain from the mainland in the 18th century, they found a fairly prosperous group of Shi'ite farmers and artisans already occupying the islands. These people owed their well-being to the fairly abundant sources of fresh water on the islands. Many of the descendents of these original inhabitants still resent the power exercised by those whom they still consider to be usurpers—who swept in, took command, and became wealthy and powerful. Various Persian and Iranian rulers have carefully nurtured this resentment and tried to use it to their advantage over the years.

The shah of Iran eventually renounced his claim on Bahrain, but Iran still wielded an enormous amount of influence over many of Bahrain's Shi'ite inhabitants. In the summer of 1979, several rather violent demonstrations led by the Bahraini Shi'ite faction were sharply put down. The situation remained fairly quiet until the failed coup attempt in December 1981, in which 81 people were arrested. Most of those taken into custody were Bahraini. It was easy to learn that the operation had been planned by Hojatolislam Hadi al-Modarris, an Iranian who had been put in charge of destabilizing the gulf. He had lived in Bahrain long enough to be considered almost a native. When another coup was prevented in 1987, his name was inevitably linked to it again. The plotters this time planned to take over as many key points and positions as possible on December 26, while the emir was out of the country.

Manama is dominantly a Sunni town, surrounded by Shi'ite villages. Some of these villages have become religious enclaves, or "islands," within the large and ever-expanding capital city. The emir is sensitive to the socioeconomic stress presented by the great imbalance of wealth and power between members of the two religious groups. Today, a number of cabinet members and a relatively high proportion of senior officials are Shi'ite.

However, Shi'ites have not been given positions in the Ministry of Defense, or the internal security departments.

Hoping to break down the barriers between the two Islamic sects, the government pushed through two major housing projects designed to become "melting pot" towns where both Shi'a and Sunni sects could live side-by-side in a comfortable fashion. Sunni and Shi'a mosques, or worship places, stand close to one another and families are intermingled. However, even though both sects live in the same vicinity, there is very little social mixing between the two communities.

Although Shi'a Muslims tend to be discriminated against in terms of achieving wealth, power, and status in Bahrain, not all of them are poor and powerless. There are several rich merchant families among them. Many professional people and members of the middle class are also Shi'ite Muslims. Additionally, Shi'ite Bahrainis come from diverse backgrounds. Many families trace their ancestry back to the Indian subcontinent. They belong to the Shi'ite group called the Baharna. There are also many Shi'ite families whose ancestors came from what is present-day Iran. Others have simply been Bahraini for longer than anyone can trace.

As for language, the main language of Bahrain is Arabic, but English is also widely spoken. Certain ethnic minority groups also speak Urdu, Farsi, or other tongues. Because so many people in the country are from other lands, a great number of languages are spoken by small numbers of people.

Bahrain's traditional devotion to Islamic law and ties to more conservative Islamic nations have slowed the development of democratic rule there. In February 2001, many Bahrainis, both men and women, voted on a national referendum that increased representative government through a new charter and an elected parliament.

5

Government and Politics

B ahrain is a constitutional traditional monarchy. The ruler, or emir, is chief of state, and like most monarchies, the position is a hereditary one. The present ruler, Hamad Isa bin Al-Khalifa, became emir in 1999 upon his father's death. Prime Minister Khalifa bin Salman Al-Khalifa has been the head of government since 1971. A National Assembly, composed of elected members, was formed in 1973; but it was then dissolved in August 1975, and its legislative powers were assumed by the cabinet. The National Action Charter created a bicameral legislature on December 23, 2000, which was approved by a referendum of February 14, 2001. A constitution was adopted in late December 2000, which calls for instituting a partially elected legislature, a constitutional monarchy, and an independent judiciary.

Bahrain has no political parties—they are, in fact, prohibited.

Senior members of Al-Khalifa and other notable families dominate political and economic decision making.

The Al-Khalifa Family

To understand Bahrani government and politics, one must understand the all-powerful role of the Al-Khalifa. This family, a branch of the Utub tribe to which the Al Sabah ruling family of Kuwait also belongs, originally settled in Zubarah, on the western coast of Qatar, in the 18th century. Zubarah is only a few miles away from Bahrain and its wealth of pearls. At the time Bahrain was still under Persian control, and the Persians were very suspicious of the Al-Khalifa settlement so close by. They attacked the Al-Khalifa at Zubarah but failed miserably in their attempt to destroy the tribe. In 1783 the Al-Khalifa, led by Ahmad bin Khalifa (later known as Ahmad the Conqueror, founder of the dynasty), mounted an expedition against the Persian garrison, expelling it from Bahrain forever. That same year they settled in Bahrain.

The Al-Khalifa family became rulers of Bahrain as a result of conquest. At the beginning there was much tension between the successors of Ahmad the Conqueror. His nephews and sons fought for the right to be next in succession. Up until then there were no hard and fast rules regarding who would follow in the footsteps of a leader. The most capable and strongest man seemed to rise to the top as the main contender. As a result, the history of Bahrain and the Al-Khalifa during the 19th century was punctuated by varying attempts to seize power. This strife came to an end when Sheikh Isa bin Ali began his reign in 1869. Since then the law of primogeniture has applied, which states that the oldest son will succeed his father. This principle is clearly stated in the first article of Bahrain's constitution.

Unlike the ruling families elsewhere in the gulf states, the Al-Khalifa did not come to power from within the dominant society. Yet its rule has been firm, and there has often been a glaring absence of traditional dialogue between the ruler and the people in Bahrain. This is not to imply that the Al-Khalifa family has become unpopular. In fact, many of the country's citizens are quite happy with the arrangement—particularly as long as conditions are stable and their own well-being is protected.

Sheikh Isa bin Ali ruled Bahrain for a long time. His forceful personality brought peace and stability to his family and to Bahrain. Eventually, though—in 1923—he was forced to abdicate (give up his throne) by the British political resident. British authorities installed his son Sheikh Hamad as Bahrain's new ruler. Most Bahrainis did not accept this enforced abdication, however, and regarded Sheikh Ali as viceroy until his father's death in 1932. To this day, any reference to Sheikh Isa bin Ali's reign gives the dates as being from 1869 to 1932.

Bahrain does not have the tremendous petroleum wealth of some of the other Persian Gulf countries. In fact, its petroleum resources are among the smallest in the region. For this reason, the Al-Khalifa are not as fabulously wealthy as ruling families elsewhere in the gulf region. But they are very conscious of the fact that Bahrain was the first gulf country to modernize and are proud of the fact that Bahrain was the first country in the region to provide a public-school education to its citizens—and for girls as well as for boys.

Bahrain is so proud of these attributes that in 1983 they decided to celebrate the bicentennial of Arab and Al-Khalifa rule in a very distinctive way. The usual celebration would have involved parades with military fanfare and fireworks. Instead, for this special occasion Bahrain chose to highlight the long-held traditions of which it is so proud. A historical conference, entitled "Bahrain Through the Ages" was organized in Manama to commemorate the 200th anniversary of Al-Khalifa rule in Bahrain. Over 70 archaeologists and historians were convened for scholarly presentations, lively debates, and heated discussions, covering all aspects of Bahrain's past. Many historical and cultural exhibitions were also planned around the same time as the conference.

The Legal System

Bahrain's legal system is based on both Islamic law (*sharia*) and English common law. The English common law influence dates back to the 1920s, when British law advisers helped institute its principles in Bahrain. According to the constitution of 1973, the judiciary is an independent and separate branch of government. However, the prime minister appoints the highest legal authority, the minister of Justice and Islamic Affairs. The emir is the highest judicial official in the land and retains the power of pardon.

Bahrain has a dual court system consisting of both civil and sharia courts. Sharia courts deal primarily with personal matters such as marriage, divorce, and inheritance. The civil court system is concerned with civil and criminal matters. There is no suffrage (voting) permitted by the Bahraini constitution; however, Bahrainis can petition the emir for relief of grievances. The emir holds a regular *majlis*, or public meetings, at which he listens to the views of citizens and accepts petitions for his intervention in dealing with the bureaucracy or some other problem. Officials of the islands' 11 municipalities follow the emir's example and hold local versions of the national majlis.

False Start Toward Democratic Government

After independence, Bahrain's ruler at the time, Sheikh Isa bin Salman Al-Khalifa, approved a new constitution and a law establishing an elected National Assembly of 30 members. The assembly met for the first time in 1973. However, after only two years of operation, the emir dissolved the legislature.

What happened? Why was democracy derailed before it

had really begun? The problem is a common one in the Middle East. It is basically a conflict between traditional tribal authority on the one hand and popular democracy where the people participate in government through elections on the other. Governmental authority in Bahrain is defined by the 1973 constitution as being hereditary—that is, succession passes down from the ruling emir to his eldest son. Bahrain is the only gulf state with this custom, and the country's emirs believe that it is their historical right to rule. Bahrain has no tradition of political parties or of representative government. When the National Assembly was established in 1973 to broaden the political process, legislative members were expected to debate laws prepared by the Council of Ministers and formulate a budget for the country. Instead, the assembly members spent most of their time arguing with each other or criticizing the ruler instead of focusing on important issues facing the nation. Disgusted with the lack of progress, the emir dissolved the assembly two years later. He said it was preventing the government from doing the work it was supposed to do.

Since 1975 Bahrain has gone back to its original patriarchal authority structure. The country enjoys great stability and peace despite its lack of democratic principles. However, the Gulf War did cause Bahrain to become more involved in regional affairs. One resulting change was the emir's formation of a *Shura*, or Council of State, in 1993. The Shura's purpose is to "initiate debate" on national social, educational, cultural, and health issues before they are codified into law. Members of the ruling family serve on the Shura, but the council also includes representatives from business and industry.

Foreign Relations

Bahrain is the smallest nation in the Persian Gulf region. It is very understandable that the country feels extremely vulnerable to powerful neighbors like Iran and Iraq. For this reason, Bahrain maintains a close and meaningful relationship with Saudi Arabia and other Arab monarchial regimes.

During the 1970s, Iraq frequently denounced Bahrain as an enemy of Arab nationalism and a puppet of American imperialism. The primary irritant was that Bahrain allowed U.S. Navy ships to establish a base in the country. Bahrainis also believe that Iraq supports opposition groups in Bahrain who repeatedly try to overthrow the Al-Khalifa dynasty. Other countries such as Iran also have criticized Bahrain's institution of monarchy as being "un-Islamic." Four separate plots were uncovered during the 1980s to overthrow the Bahraini regime—and it is believed that all were inspired by Iran.

The 1980s Iran-Iraq War caused Bahrain to lobby other Arab monarchies in the gulf region to cooperate in defense matters. Once fighting had broken out between Iran and Iraq, the Persian Gulf was so destabilized that Kuwait, Qatar, the United Arab Emirates, Oman, and Saudi Arabia joined Bahrain in forming the Gulf Cooperation Council (GCC). At first this agreement emphasized economic cooperation, but every year the importance of security issues grew. The countries participated in joint training maneuvers and beefed up their armed forces. Compared to their size and population, Bahrain and the other members of the GCC spend lavishly on what they believe to be their military needs. Nevertheless, their small areas and populations as well as their many ethnic divisions keep them from being able to mount a strong defense should they be threatened. They also have very limited experience in the effective use of modern weapons and an extremely small area in which to practice using them.

When Iraq invaded Kuwait in 1990, Bahrain joined the collective military effort against Iraq by sending a small contingent of troops to the front lines in Saudi Arabia. It also allowed the United States to use its naval and air facilities.

When Bahrain allowed the U.S. Navy to establish a base there in the 1970s, Iraq denounced the Bahraini leadership as puppets of American imperialism. Many believe that subsequent plots to overthrow the Bahraini government can be traced to Iraq and Iran.

Friends and Allies

Bahrain maintains friendly relations with most countries within the Persian Gulf region. Iraq is the one exception, and that country is kept at arm's length. Bahrain also maintains friendly relations with several countries outside the region, its closest links being with Great Britain and the United States. After the Persian Gulf War, Bahrain signed a defense cooperation agreement with the United States, allowing the U.S. to use Bahrain's military facilities and stockpile military supplies and equipment in Bahrain. Even though Bahrain, along with the other GCC members, wanted to be independent and meet their own defense needs, they realized that they needed the involvement of the western powers. Now a new security framework is in place in the gulf region. Bahrain and the other GCC nations are allied with the United States, Great Britain, and France, and these nations provide a strategic security umbrella over the gulf region to ensure peace and protect shipping lanes. The United States and Great Britain still staff naval stations in Bahrain and in the gulf but do not plan to station permanent troops there.

Bahrain is a member of several international organizations, including the United Nations (UN), the International Monetary Fund (IMF), and the World Health Organization (WHO). It also belongs to several regional organizations such as the League of Arab Nations, the Organization of Petroleum Exporting Countries (OPEC), and the Organization of the Islamic Conference.

Matters of Regional Security

Although relatively peaceful itself, Bahrain is located in one of the world's most strategic and troubled regions. The country seems to be threatened constantly by forces beyond its boundary and control. When the Iranian Revolution broke out in 1979, the entire Persian Gulf region was threatened and destabilized. The following year fighting broke out between Iran and Iraq, and the gulf's oil industry and shipping capabilities were threatened. Bahrain, Kuwait, and other countries in the region feared that this war would spread to their own countries.

Deep concerns also were fueled by Iran's revolutionary image of Islamic fundamentalism. Iran's radical talk inflamed some of Bahrain's religious leaders, many students, and also many of the country's poor and less educated citizens. As tensions in the area grew, Bahrain discovered a small band of revolutionaries hiding in their nation, a group dedicated to the overthrow of traditional Arab regimes. Iran's religious leader, the Ayatollah Khomeini, allegedly masterminded a plot to topple Bahrain's government in December 1981. However, Iran's president, Seyyed Ali Khameni, denied that Iran had any role in the sabotage of Bahrain. He further insisted that Israel had created the situation in Bahrain as a means of diverting attention from its annexation of the Golan Heights from Syria.

Another great blow to the region occurred in August 1990, when Iraq invaded Kuwait. Suddenly there was a very real possibility that Iraqi forces would continue southward along the gulf coast in an attempt to seize other oil-rich Arab states. Bahrain joined the other smaller Arab countries in offering their airfields and ports as bases for the forces of Operation Desert Storm to defeat Iraq.

Traditional rivalries and territorial disputes between Bahrain and the other Arab Persian Gulf states still exist, but they are becoming less important as sources of tension. Terrorist problems stemming from Iran have dwindled, and foreign workers are carefully monitored to prevent foreign influences from causing unrest. Bahrain's police force rigidly controls internal dissent that could cause instability in the region. However, members of the conservative ruling families steadfastly resist democratic reforms, and this has the potential to cause future problems in Bahrain and the region.

Although Bahrain's production of oil is not large when compared to some of it neighbors, it nonetheless contributes more than half of the country's export earnings.

6

The Economy

Bahrain is crowded and growing but doing quite well. Its residents enjoy one of the highest standards of living in the Persian Gulf region, and individual family incomes are quite high by regional standards. The country's economy is strong enough to ensure that most families have jobs and make enough money to provide for their basic comfort and needs. The country has access to adequate supplies of clean water, people eat well, and good nutrition along with a generous supply of doctors and excellent health-care facilities have combined to give Bahrainis long and healthy lives. Bahraini citizens also receive a decent level of free public education. It is little wonder that Bahrain is the envy of many of its neighbors in the region.

Because of its small area and lack of environmental diversity, Bahrain has limited natural resources; however, over the centuries it has made the most of its few opportunities. Its most important resources have always been of a liquid nature. First, for centuries the gulf yielded an abundance of pearls and fish as well as sailing access to distant lands. Today it is the source of desalinized water that provides over half of Bahrain's supply for both domestic and agricultural irrigation use. Second, there are the scattered freshwater oases around which people and farms have clustered for thousands of years. Finally, there is petroleum, which provides more than half of Bahrain's export earnings.

Primary Industries

A primary industry is one that takes direct advantage of natural resources. Examples include fishing, farming, mining, and logging. The first three of these industries have played a very important role in Bahrain's economy.

Resources of the Gulf. Beautiful pearls have been gathered for thousands of years from the Persian Gulf's oyster beds. The gulf in general, and the waters surrounding Bahrain in particular, produce the world's best natural pearls. These precious jewels form in oysters, and the oyster-rich waters around Bahrain yielded enough shellfish to support anyone interested in pearl diving as a way of making a living. Harvesting pearls is a very difficult task, but the techniques have improved greatly over the centuries. Modern scuba equipment, for example, now allows divers to go much deeper and to remain under water for much greater periods of time.

Until the 1930s pearling was Bahrain's major industry and source of income. During its peak, more than a quarter of the country's population was engaged in the industry. Some 2,000 *dhows* (sailboats) were involved in the activity, which reached its peak during the warm-water months of June through October. In the early 1930s, however, pearling fell into a sharp decline. Three things combined to bring this about. First, during the worldwide Great Depression, few people could afford such luxuries and the market plummeted. Second, the

Fishing remains a key source of both income and food in Bahrain. Traditionally, much of the fishing in Bahrain has been done using small vessels called *dhows*. Government aid to the fishing industry since the 1980s has helped modernize the commercial fishing fleet and meet increased demand.

Japanese developed the cultured pearl industry—they learned how to "grow" pearls in oysters under artificial conditions—and through this technique, the market was suddenly flooded with less-expensive yet still high quality gems, and the value of natural pearls crashed. Finally, in the 1930s oil production began in Bahrain, and many people decided that working the oil fields was easier, safer, and a more reliable source of income than diving for pearls.

More than 200 varieties of fish live in the gulf waters surrounding Bahrain. For centuries fishing was an important source of both income and diet. Fishing, too, died out as an important contributor to the country's economy at about the same time that the pearling industry crashed.

By the early 1980s consumer demand for fish was increasing. But Bahrain was faced with the paradox of being fish rich (as a natural resource) but having to import nearly all of its seafood. Recognizing the problem, the government began a program to redevelop the fishing industry. It helped fishermen replace the old dhow fleets with modern boats and motors, and replaced traditional fish traps made of woven palm fronds with modern wire mesh traps. These efforts were successful, and Bahrain is once again harvesting its rich fishery resources.

Agriculture. Only about 1 percent of the land in Bahrain is suitable for farming and today agriculture accounts for less than 2 percent of the country's total gross domestic product (GDP). Historically, however, agriculture's contribution to the region has been significant. Early farming settlements clustered around the natural freshwater springs and these early oases were very important to Bahrain's early settlement and economic development.

Date palms, in particular, were a very important crop. The palms produce dates, of course—a tasty, nutritious, and very durable dried fruit that was eaten locally and also exported. In addition to the fruit, all other parts of the palm also are useful for some purpose: The wood is used for fuel and building; the fronds (leaves) are used for thatching and provide shade; even the buds and flowers are used in various ways.

Unfortunately, as groundwater becomes increasingly saline (salty), farmland is becoming less productive. During recent decades, many Bahrainis have left the land and small agricultural villages and moved to Manama and its suburbs. The abandoned farmland often is neglected, left to return to its original desert condition. Today there are just over 2,000 farmers, nearly three-fourths of whom do not own the land on which they work. The ruling Al-Khalifa family, of course, owns the greatest acreage and most productive land.

Petroleum. In 1932 Bahrain became the first Persian Gulf

state to strike oil. Production, however, has never been large. During recent years, Bahrain's daily production of crude oil has been less than 40,000 barrels. By comparison, the neighboring United Arab Emirates produce about 2 million barrels each day. Nonetheless, petroleum contributes more than half the country's export earnings. Bahrain also produces natural gas, all of which is used domestically. In the late 1990s several American oil companies signed agreements with the Bahraini government to undertake further exploration in the offshore waters controlled by the country.

Manufacturing and Processing Industries

Because of its limited oil production, Bahrain has developed a much more diversified economy than have states in the gulf region. In the early 1960s the country began to diversify its industries from simple oil production to petroleum refining, petrochemicals, aluminum production, and ship repair. Today it is home to the largest aluminum smelter in the Middle East and one of the region's largest shipbuilding and repair yards. The huge BAPCO oil refinery—the oldest in the gulf region, built in 1936—has a daily production capacity of 260,000 barrels and is being expanded. Petroleum comes by pipeline from oil-rich Saudi Arabia, just 14 miles (25 kilometers) away. These industries, and the allied service-related businesses, provide adequate jobs not only for Bahrainis but also for many internationals that flock to the country seeking employment.

The government continues to introduce policies designed to encourage economic growth. Foreigners, for example, are permitted to own onshore companies, and the government steadfastly refuses to tax corporate or personal income.

Financial Services

Many factors have combined to make Bahrain the leading international banking and financial center in the Middle East. The government actively seeks foreign investment as it works to make the country an even greater center of finance, trade, and service. Among the advantages it cites are:

- A stable, progressive, liberal government that supports private ownership

- A history of peace and prosperity

- A hardworking, enterprising, well educated population

- A well-established and fair legal system

- Excellent communications, telecommunications, and transportation

- Abundant energy supplies

- A strategic geographical location

Bahrain's legal system is designed to protect capital investments, so businesses do not hesitate to pour money into the nation. Laws foster a stable business environment in which local businessmen and international companies can invest and grow. Companies, in turn, are expected to cooperate with the government by obeying its laws. Bahrain's strategic location in the Persian Gulf region and its reputation as a banking center have also put it at the forefront. Many international companies are establishing offices in the country.

Location, again, has played a very important role in Bahrain's development as a leading financial center. Approximately 150 banks and other financial services—including nearly all Arab financial institutions—are established in the country. With its strategic longitudinal location between eastern and western time zones and its advanced digital telecommunications systems, Bahrain is able to communicate with nearly all the world's major financial centers in the course of a business day. Additionally, many branches of foreign insurance companies, law firms, public relations consultants, and financial analysts also have offices here. Adoption of the *dinar* as the country's currency spurred the growth of Bahrain's banking system. The dinar is a freely convertible and stable currency that is firmly linked to the U.S. dollar.

Tourism

Tourism is one of Bahrain's most rapidly expanding industries. In 2000 it accounted for slightly over 10 percent of the country's income and employed about 18 percent of the workforce.

Currently, some three million tourists visit the country, and the numbers grow annually. Tourists are attracted by Bahrain's western-style shopping malls, theaters, hotels, and restaurants as well as by the availability of alcoholic beverages and golf courses (with green grass!). Parks, museums, historical sites, and "green" (ecological) tourism opportunities also draw thousands of visitors.

Communication and Transportation

One of the reasons that Bahrain is able to attract large-scale foreign investment and activity is because of its superb transportation and communication facilities. The country possesses one of the world's most advanced digital telecommunications systems. Individuals and businesses have access to exclusive private channels, international databases, and the Internet.

Bahrain International Airport is the busiest center of commercial aviation in the Persian Gulf region. It handles approximately 3 million passengers a year, about half of whom are making connections with other flights going to further destinations. The modern facility was built to accommodate up to 10 million passengers a year—a sign that Bahrain is very optimistic about the role of air travel in its future. The country also possesses an excellent road system, and since Bahrain is so small, it is not hard to get around. The bus system is very dependable, and visitors can even rent cars to travel around the islands at their own leisure.

In December 1986 the King Faud Causeway opened, linking

The opening of a causeway between Bahrain and the Saudi Arabian mainland in 1986 has brought flocks of Saudi tourists to Bahrain's hotels and restaurants, while allowing Bahrainis to shop on the mainland.

Bahrain to the eastern mainland of Saudi Arabia. Many Bahrainis had believed that such a link would cause a loss of isolation and independence, so while Saudi Arabia had promised to finance the causeway, the Bahrainis dragged their feet as long as they could. Even though only 15 miles (24 kilometers) separate Bahrain from Saudi Arabia, Bahrain appreciated the uniqueness and independence of their island status.

The causeway has received mixed reviews since it opened. Hotel and restaurant owners are its biggest fans, and flocks of Saudi weekend tourists have helped to take up the slack of the post-oil boom. Some Bahraini merchants have been less happy. The causeway has made it very easy for Bahrainis to shop on the Saudi mainland. Anything from food to car parts can be brought back duty free. Larger Saudi markets and Saudi price subsidies mean that prices are on average 30 percent lower there than in Bahrain. Island merchants can no longer justify their inflated prices. Costs have been lowered to be competitive and encourage Bahraini shoppers to buy at home rather than driving across the causeway for minor purchases.

Most Bahrainis are happy to have easy access to the Saudi mainland. But there have been a few problems associated with the causeway. After it opened, for example, the number of brawls and other aggressive acts grew sharply. Many Bahrainis also feared that once the countries were linked, Saudis would exert pressures on Bahrain to change its liberal social laws related to alcohol and public entertainment. While this has not yet happened, Bahrainis still feel that they are under close watch. On the other hand, during the war between nearby Iran and Iraq, Bahrainis were glad to exchange some freedom for protection. The causeway provided a guarantee that the Saudi army could be in Manama within several hours if the need arose.

Workforce

Bahrain's workforce is highly literate and well trained. There are also many foreigners who claim residence in another country but work for wages in Bahrain. They send most of their paychecks home to their families and usually hold the most menial and low-paying jobs. The government has instituted many programs and incentives to draw more Bahrainis into the workforce. The number of women working outside the home has risen sharply over the past few decades, in part because of government incentive programs. In fact, Bahrain has more women in the workforce than any other country in the Persian Gulf region. Many are single. They plan to work perhaps two to five years after finishing their education before leaving their jobs to marry and start a family. In an effort to encourage women to continue working outside the home after marriage, the government has enacted laws that help working mothers. They receive paid maternity leave and other benefits, and the law strictly forbids any form of discrimination against them.

A program to redevelop the fishing industry has forced the replacement of the traditional *dhow* fleets with modern boats and motors. Children of the skilled artisans who built the *dhows* are choosing other means of making a living.

7

Living in Bahrain Today

Were you to visit Bahrain today, much of what you saw and experienced would make you feel quite at home. Cities are modern, stores are full of familiar items, and there are many opportunities for Western-style entertainment. Many American franchises have outlets there, including some hotels and restaurants. Their airport is world class as are their various communications and financial institutions. Jobs are similar to those we know, as well. Both the United States and Bahrain have fewer than 2 percent of their populations engaged in farming, with most people in both countries engaged in service industries. Whereas Arabic is Bahrain's main language, a large percentage of the people also speak English, which is a required second language in the schools.

Only when you looked beneath the surface would differences in our respective ways of living become apparent. And these differences—such as religion and social customs—are the result of our two distinctly different cultures. In this chapter you will learn more about Bahrain's culture and the day-to-day way that its people live.

A Conservative Society

Bahrainis are very conservative. Theirs is a very private society; signs of emotion or affection are rarely shown in public, and their feelings are kept to themselves. Even laughing and joking are rarely heard in public. Arguments or disagreements between spouses, friends, or people in general also are kept very private. The importance of privacy is evident in the architecture of Bahraini houses, which are built with thick and solid walls. In building and furnishing, great care is taken to ensure that strangers or neighbors cannot see into the house.

Family Structure and Duties

Although their country has become increasingly modernized during recent decades, most Bahrainis have retained a number of traditional Arab ways. Family life, for example, is greatly influenced by their Bedouin tribal past and their Islamic faith. Islamic beliefs and laws form the foundation of Bahrain's customs, laws, and practices.

Gender and age play a major role in Bahraini families. The father is the family head and provider of material needs in most traditional households. Traditional Islamic culture stresses the importance of women's role in taking care of the house and raising children. In recent years, however, it has become increasingly common for both parents to hold jobs and for servants and/or maids to care for the household. And today in most families, both parents make important decisions jointly.

Women in Bahrain have greater freedom than in many other Middle Eastern countries—indeed, greater freedom for women is a direct result of free education available to both sexes. They shop in markets in small groups, and occasionally even alone—a sight never seen in the more conservative Islamic states. They stop at juice stalls and chat or window shop, many times without wearing the *abbaya,* a black cloaklike garment. Very few women veil their faces. Bahraini women do not hesitate to enter a restaurant—at least one of the more expensive ones—and are often found working in banks, shops, hospitals, television stations, and offices.

Social Life

Bahrainis are a very social people. When someone returns from a trip, relatives, friends, and neighbors will drop by with a greeting. If a Bahraini is sick and confined to home or hospital, many visitors will stop by to offer moral support or simply to be of some company—and usually they will be bearing the customary food, chocolates, fruits, or flowers. When people marry, their relatives, friends, and neighbors will bring gifts of money or household items. After having a baby, a woman usually spends the first 40 days in her family's home, where her mother and sisters care for her.

A visit to a Bahraini home would start with positioning yourself by the front door in such a spot that you are unable to see inside the house. If the host gestures to you with a right palm up, you are welcome to come inside. Most homes have a special room, called a *majlis* or *dewaniah,* which is used for entertaining guests. It is located close to the front of the house and near the outside main entrance. Women guests may gather in another room, sometimes entered through a special outside entrance used only by women. Guests are not expected to bring food or other gifts if invited to a dewaniah. Some dewaniahs are furnished with couches, but traditional ones have no furniture, and everyone sits on Persian rugs. If invited to a Bahraini home, always use only your right hand for eating, and never point the soles of your feet toward anyone because this is seen as an insult!

Bahraini culture stresses the importance of honoring

Bahraini social culture remains grounded in ritual. As elsewhere around the world, sharing a cup of coffee is a traditional national pastime.

guests and pampering them. The host will do everything possible to make certain that guests are comfortable. Food will be served in excessive amounts until every guest is satisfied. If the host has finished before the others, he will act as though he is still eating until all guests are finished. In this manner the host makes sure that his guests do not feel rushed into finishing. Neither alcohol nor pork will be served in a traditional Muslim home because it is against the Islamic faith to consume these items.

Drinking coffee is a traditional Bahraini welcoming gesture. The coffee ceremony begins with preparation. Three cupfuls of water and a rounded teaspoonful of coffee are poured into a saucepan and then boiled for about two minutes. Next comes the relaxation process, which gives the coffee time to brew while the traditional greetings and welcome are exchanged. Saffron in rosewater and cardamom may be added to the coffee. After brewing for 5 to 10 minutes, the coffee is served in a small cup. It is polite to accept a second cup if offered, but if you have had enough, it is polite to shake your cup from side to side.

Clothing and Dress

In accordance with Islamic law, traditionally Bahraini women must be covered from head to toe when in public. In the city, many women wear a black cloaklike abbaya over modern clothes. For special occasions, they will wear more colorful clothing decorated with gold embroidery. A village woman generally wears a *thobe,* a long dress over baggy pants. A man's traditional clothing is a full-length coat, either of dark wool for winter or white cotton for summer. They also wear *servwaal,* light cotton trousers that resemble baggy pajama pants, under their coats. For special occasions, they often wear a *bisht* (cloak) made of beige or black wool and trimmed with gold embroidery. Men usually wear a crocheted cap topped with a head scarf. The scarf is held in place by a black wool headband.

If you are a woman visiting Bahrain, you, too, will need to cover up! Foreign women must wear long skirts that cover their legs, and they are not permitted to wear two-piece bathing suits at the beach.

The *Ma'atam*

The most typical institution of Bahraini Shi'ism is the *ma'atam,* or prayer room. The faithful gather in their ma'atam to listen to the tragic chants that retrace over and over again the life and death of several great Shi'a martyrs. For conservative families living in rural villages, the ma'atam is the center of their life outside the home. It is the social hall, school, and meeting place all rolled into one. Families are extremely loyal

Bahraini standards of dress still adhere to the tenets of Islamic law. Many women must wear veils and remain covered from head to toe when in public.

and faithful to a specific ma'atam. In traditional culture, even marriages are decided within the community of the ma'atam. Whereas there may be several ma'atams within a village, there is virtually no interaction between them. The fact that they are so numerous and generate such a fierce loyalty makes ma'atams as much a factor of social division as of unity.

Although nearly all Bahrainis are Muslim, people in the

country are free to practice other religions, such as Christianity, Judaism, Bahai, Hinduism, or Parsi. The ruling family of Bahrain, the Al-Khalifa, considers it one of their most important tasks to ensure their Shi'ite subjects do not fight among themselves or with their Sunni neighbors.

Education

Bahrain is extremely proud of the fact that it has the oldest public-education system in the Arabian Peninsula. The first public boys' school opened in 1919, and, more surprisingly, the first public school for girls opened only 10 years later. The government is very committed to education and spends a large portion of its revenue on improving schooling—however, education is not mandatory. Some conservative villagers do not want their daughters educated. They are afraid that by going to school, their daughters' minds will be filled with strange ideas that may be in conflict with their own beliefs. This attitude is becoming less popular, however, as Bahrain now has one of the highest literacy rates in the Arab world and the highest female literacy rate in the gulf region (literacy rate refers to the percentage of people age 15 and over who can read and write). The adult literacy rate stands at 90 percent for males and 80 percent for females.

Public-school education is free in Bahrain. Students receive supplies, uniforms, meals, and transportation to and from school at no charge. Almost all children from ages 6 to 11 attend school, and about two-thirds of all 12 to 14-year olds are enrolled in intermediate schools. However, many girls drop out of school after they reach the age of 14. In addition to public schools, there are several private and religious schools in Bahrain. The Bahrain International School is an accredited private academy operated by the United States, offering classes from elementary through secondary levels. While the majority of Bahrain's teachers are native-born, the largest group of foreign teachers comes from Egypt.

The country has two universities. The University of Bahrain was created in 1986 with the merger of two smaller colleges. Its more than 5,000 students, half of whom are women, can select from a wide variety of academic subjects. The island is also home to the Arabian Gulf University. This much smaller institution was founded in 1984 and is funded by the six member countries of the Gulf Cooperation Council (GCC): Kuwait, Oman, Qatar, the United Arab Emirates, and Saudi Arabia. Its medical school is the largest in the gulf region.

Health Care

Bahrain has offered free health care to its citizens since 1925. The government provides free immunization programs and free hospitalization. Citizens also receive general medical, dental, optical, psychiatric, and both maternity and pediatric care free of charge. Bahrainis generally enjoy the best health in the region and have a life expectancy comparable to that of many Western countries: 71 years for men and 75.5 for women. Even foreign visitors and workers in Bahrain can receive free medical services during their stay. Bahrain established a social security system in 1976. Only Bahraini citizens are eligible for retirement pensions, but both residents and foreign workers are covered against accidents.

Leisure-Time Activities

Bahrain is *the* place to go in the Persian Gulf region when you want to attend a rock concert, an opera, or a ballet! The country has become an entertainment center, presenting both cultural and sporting events. Bahraini hotels offer entertainment that is on the same level as that offered in large American cities. Hotels provide a main source of entertainment outside of family activities. Attractive women from Thailand and the Philippines work as hostesses in the hotel bars. However, they must abide by the dress code for foreign women, so their skirts extend down to their ankles, and their manner is prim and proper. Arab musical stars as well as international theater actors and exhibition sports matches are all part of the available entertainment.

Bahrain has excellent facilities, such as a 4,000-seat indoor theater, several conference centers, and major outdoor arenas. These lavish entertainment centers as well as Bahrain's relative social freedom have helped make the country a major regional tourism center—indeed, weekend visits, especially from Saudi visitors, provide a welcome and substantial source of income for Bahrain. It also is becoming an increasingly popular site for international conferences of business people or scholars.

As time and tradition move into a new millennium, modern cellphone technology and the ancient art of falconry coexist in Bahrain.

8

Bahrain Looks Ahead

B ahrain appears to have a bright future. Its people enjoy the most cosmopolitan, safe, and relaxed lifestyle available in the Persian Gulf. Their country has become the "Economic Gateway to the Gulf," and the government is working hard to attract information technology and other "clean" industries. Several world-class computer and software companies already have chosen Bahrain as their regional base for sales and support operations. During recent decades, the government has built at least 10 industrial areas to accommodate over 500 different manufacturing and service companies.

Bahrainis like to think of their country as the Singapore or Hong Kong of the Persian Gulf, seasoned with a dash of Monaco. Like Singapore, Bahrain is also a small island state. Also like Singapore, Bahrain has become an important regional center for financial and other services. The comparison to Hong Kong is that of another small, dynamic nation working alongside a slower but powerful giant.

Finally, Monaco is a fun-loving place of great pleasures, and the Persian Gulf appreciates such pleasures of life, too.

Bahrain was the first gulf state to find and export oil and to benefit from the oil age. Its first commercial well came on stream in 1932, and the first oil-laden tanker steamed out in December 1933. But it is also the first gulf state that has been forced to consider life after oil. Its wells are nearly exhausted. Since the height of the oil boom, Bahrain has thought about how it can profit from its neighbors' oil. Fortunately, the country has several other assets on which it can capitalize.

The first major asset that Bahrain possesses is its geographic location. As the economic gateway to the Persian Gulf, it is surrounded by vast petroleum wealth and opportunity. What could be more sensible than to make an archipelago in the middle of the gulf a world-class communications center or center of offshore banking?

Another advantage Bahrain has is its population. Its official 2000 population was 634,137 (some population estimates are as high as 700,000), an estimated three-quarters of whom are Bahrainis. This relatively large native population presents both strengths and problems. The population is more homogeneous than in most Arab countries. But, Bahrain cannot use the safety valve of sending surplus expatriate labor home in case of reduced labor demand. With the global economic downturn of the 1990s, Bahrain's economy has also suffered a slump. It is the first country in the gulf where many of its young citizens have experienced difficulties in finding a job.

The third asset is the educational level of its citizens. Bahrain can boast of having the highest percentage of educated people in the gulf region. Much of the prestige enjoyed by Bahrainis is based on their reputation as educated people. They are widely considered to be a population of intellectuals.

Finally, one of Bahrain's chief assets is the presence of an atmosphere of freedom and liberty. Many things not found elsewhere in the Persian Gulf are available in Bahrain. Alcohol,

Bahrain is among the more liberal of the Islamic nations in its social attitudes, particularly toward women. They may have careers outside the home.

for example, is freely available. Anyone who wants to drink can do so, without any questions being asked about religion or nationality. It is an important freedom that attracts many visitors from elsewhere in the Muslim world. Many Muslims drink alcohol, even though strictly forbidden by the Qur'an *(Koran)*, or holy book of Islam. Another freedom that Bahrainis enjoy is found in the relative ease with which women can move in society. Many women work outside the home. They enjoy the freedom to work in offices, shops, and hotels. There are no restrictions on working in jobs that involve normal contact with men.

The freedom of which Bahrainis are justifiably proud applies mainly to individual behavior. The idea of an individual being able to choose how to behave is totally alien to society on the Arabian Peninsula, whereas in Bahrain, if a person exercises discretion in behavior, he or she can have as much individual freedom as is desired. Public and civil liberties, however, are not as freely found in Bahrain. Press, radio, and television are closely monitored and often censored by the Ministry of Information. Many of Bahrain's neighbors enjoy considerably more freedom of the press. Foreign journalists are promptly expelled if the Ministry of Information feels they have stepped out of line— and it does not matter if they work for the local newspaper or an international relief agency.

Because Bahrain is such a small nation and is positioned close to other patriarchal-governed states, it appears that democratic reforms will come very slowly. The country's short experiment with an elected parliament in 1973 ended with its closing in 1975, and newly formed political parties were outlawed at the same time. Now there is no talk of bringing political parties back, even from a few representatives of opposition groups in exile.

Anything that threatens the tribal legacy will collide with the ruling elite and be quickly squelched. Since Sheikh Hamad bin Isa Al-Khalifa became emir in 1999 after the death of his father, the social unrest over proposed reforms has quieted down. The emir has repeatedly stressed his commitment to developing democracy in Bahrain, and Bahrainis are anxiously awaiting anticipated improvements.

In February 2001 Sheikh Hamad permitted a public referendum, or vote, to be held. A major issue voted on was whether Bahrain should be transformed from an absolute monarchy to a constitutional monarchy. They also voted on whether to establish a parliament with two chambers, one of which was to be directly elected. Another issue voted on was the establishment of an independent judiciary. Right before the vote, the emir pardoned more than 900 political prisoners and exiles to ensure that Bahrain received the praise of human rights agencies and groups. The vote went overwhelmingly in support of the political reforms listed. Within days, they began making at least some of the changes voted by the country's people.

Despite the many changes currently happening in Bahrain, there is one key reality: The ruling family has been in power for more than two centuries, and this system is deeply embedded in Bahraini society. Some outside observers have been quite critical of recent developments, calling them "cosmetic" or "superficial." The emir and the prime minister, they point out, would still appoint members to the upper house of the parliament that in turn would hold veto power over the elected chamber. It is most doubtful that the emir, or the ruling Al-Khalifa family, would give up their control over Bahrain.

Most observers, however, believe that the reforms are a positive step toward democratization. The current practice of holding weekly *majlises* (public assemblies) gives the people ready access to the emir. They can bring their grievances to him and request his intervention during these meetings. However, the educated professional classes will undoubtedly continue to exert pressure for representative government. Already some of the changes they pressed for have been implemented. In 1995 the first cabinet shakeup in 20 years occurred. The ruling family's membership in the cabinet was reduced to seven of the 16 seats, thereby making it a minority.

Bahrain's relations with its gulf neighbors are generally good. Tensions between the country and Iran seem to be relaxing; in fact, the two countries have reached an agreement to exchange ambassadors. (However, Bahrain still accuses Iran of sponsoring subversive terrorist activities in the country. Old suspicions die hard, and it will take time for Bahrain to become convinced that Iran has lost its desire to invade and take control of this island state.) Also, the long-running dispute between Bahrain and Qatar over the Hawar Islands may be close to being resolved. Bahrain has controlled these islands since the 1930s.

Bahrain has a very bright future. It enjoys a strategic location, it is well governed, and it has the region's most diversified economy. Its people are well educated and enjoy many benefits not shared by most others in the region, including many more individual freedoms. Of greatest importance perhaps is that the country and its people are quite flexible. They can adjust rapidly to conditions in an ever-changing world without losing their own identity.

Facts at a Glance

Land and People

Official Name of Country State of Bahrain

Location Middle East, archipelago in the Persian Gulf, east of Saudi Arabia

Area 267 square miles (692 square kilometers)

Climate Arid; mild, pleasant winters; very hot, humid summers

Highest Point Jabal ad Dukhan (440 feet; 134 meters)

Lowest Point Persian Gulf (0 meters)

Capital Manama

Population Approximately 700,000 (2002 estimate)

Official Language Arabic

Other Major Languages English, Farsi, Urdu

Ethnic Groups Bahraini 63 percent, Asian 19 percent, other Arab 10 percent, Iranian 8 percent

Literacy Rate 85%

Religions Shi'a Muslim 75 percent, Sunni Muslim 25 percent

Average Life 72 years Expectancy

Economy

Natural Resources Oil, associated and nonassociated natural gas, fish

Land Use Arable land: 1 percent; permanent crops: 1 percent; permanent pastures: 6 percent; forests and woodland: 0 percent; desert: 92 percent. Irrigated land 10 square kilometers (1993 estimate)

Major Imports Crude petroleum, machinery, transportation equipment, food

Major Exports Crude oil, refined oil products, aluminum

Major Trading Saudi Arabia, India, United States, Japan, United Arab Emirates Partners

Agricultural Products Eggs, vegetables, dates, dairy, poultry

Currency Bahraini dinar

Government

Form of Government Traditional monarchy

Legislature Cabinet-executive system

Political Party None permitted

Head of Government Prime Minister Khalifa bin Salman Al-Khalifa

Head of State Amir Hamad bin Isa Al-Khalifa (since March 5, 1999)

Cabinet Appointed by the monarch

Elections None; the monarch is hereditary; prime minister appointed by monarch

3200–200 B.C.	Formative Dilmun. First mentioned in Mesopotamian inscriptions.
2200–1600 B.C.	Early Dilmun. Golden age of prosperity and influence.
1600–1000 B.C.	Middle Dilmun. Mesopotamia under Kassite rule.
1000–330 B.C.	Late Dilmun. Decline of copper trade and switch to trade in spices and incense.
1500s A.D.	Portugese seized Bahrain as a trading post to protect their monopoly over the spice trade.
1604–1782	Periodic occupation by Bahrain after Portuguese ousted.
1783	Al-Khalifa family seizes power over all other tribes and groups.
1880	Bahrain becomes a British protectorate.
1971	Bahrain gains its independence.
1973–1975	New Constitution establishes a Constituent Assembly, but the ruler dissolves it shortly thereafter.
1990s	Territorial disputes with Qatar. Bahrain takes aggressive steps to revive and diversify its economy.
1991	Bahrain participates in Operation Desert Storm as part of the Gulf Cooperation Council (GCC); Bahrain signs a defense cooperation pact with the United States.
1996	Coup attempt plot uncovered by an Iranian-backed group, Hezbollah. Bahrain recalls its ambassador to Iran.
1998	Bahrain provides military facilities for Operation Desert Fox, a U.S. and British bombing campaign against Iraq. Emir of Bahrain visits Qatar to resolve disputes.
2000	Emir promises to restore a democratically elected parliament after a break of 25 years. Emir also pardons over 900 political prisoners and exiles.

Bibliography

Bradshaw, Michael. *The New Global Order: World Regional Geography,* 2nd ed. (New York: McGraw-Hill Higher Education, 2002).

English, Paul, *Geography: People and Places in a Changing World,* 2nd ed. (St. Paul, Minn.: West Publishing Company, 1997).

Sager, Robert J., and David Helgren. *World Geography Today.* (New York: Holt, Rinehart and Winston, 1997).

Said, Edward. *Culture and Imperialism.* (New York: Vintage Books, 1994).

Salter, Christopher, et al. *Essentials of World Regional Geography,* 3rd ed. (Orlando, Fla: Saunders College Publishing, 2000).

Zahlan, Rosemarie Said. *The Making of the Modern Gulf States.* London: Unwin Hyman, 1989.

Index

Index

About the Author

CAROL ANN GILLESPIE teaches World Regional Geography and East Asian Studies at Grove City College in Grove City, Pennsylvania. She resides in Cranberry Township, Pennsylvania, with her husband, Michael, and her three sons.

CHARLES F. "FRITZ" GRITZNER is Distinguished Professor of Geography at South Dakota State University. He is now in his fifth decade of college teaching and research. Much of his career work has focused on geographic education. Fritz has served as both president and executive director of the National Council for Geographic Education and has received the Council's George J. Miller Award for Distinguished Service.